P9-EDA-681

Beijing in a Nutshell
Beijing im Fokus
Beijing et ses merveilles

海洋出版社

CONTENTS
INHALT
TABLE DES MATIERES

Foreword	Vorwort
Tian'anmen	Das Tian'anmen-Tor
Palace Museum	Der Kaiserpalast
Beihai Park	Der Beihai-Park
Summer Palace	Der Sommerpalast
Temple of Heaven	Der Himmelstempel
Grand View Garden	Daguanyuan
Great Wall	Die Große Mauer
Ming Tombs	Die Ming-Gräber
Residence of Prince Gong	Residenz des Prinzen Gong
Ruins of Yuanmingyuan	Die Ruinen des Yuanmingyuan
Yonghegong Lamasery	Yonghegong
Great Bell Temple	Dazhongsi
Fragrant Hills Park	Xiangshan-Park

Avant-propos 4 5 6

La porte Tian'anmen 9

Le Palais impérial 17

Le parc Beihai 33

Le Palais d'Eté 47

Le Temple du Ciel 63

Le Jardin aux Spectacles grandioses 77

La Grande Muraille 87

Les Treize Tombeaux des Ming 97

La Résidence du prince Gong 105

Ruines de Yuanmingyuan 111

La Lamaserie Yonghe 117

Le Temple de la Grande Cloche 127

La Colline parfumée 133

Foreword

Beijing, the capital of the People's Republic of China, is a world-famous historical and cultural city.

Three thousand years ago Beijing was called Ji, an important town in north China. During the Spring and Autumn, and Warring States Periods (770-221B.C.), it became the capital of the State of Yan. In the early 10th century the Liao Dynasty (907-1125) designated it its secondary capital, named Nanjing (Southern Capital),or Yanjing. In the mid-12th century the Jin Dynasty (1115-1234) established their main capital at Yanjing and named it Zhongdu (Central Capital), after which many dynasties had their capital here. The Yuan Dynasty (1271-1368) changed Zhongdu to Dadu (Great Capital),until in 1403 Zhu Di, the fourth son of Zhu Yuanzhang, the founder of the Ming Dynasty (1368-1644), became the third emperor and moved the court from Nanjing to Dadu and renamed the city Beijing (Northern Capital). On October 1,1949 the People's Republic of China was founded, and Beijing became its capital and political, economical, communications, scientific and cultural center.

Beijing is located at the northern end of the vast North China Plain, on the northwest surrounded by mountains and on the southeast by plains. Its geographical setting of mountains to the north and plains to the south has made it a place contested by the strategists of past dynasties and a modern communications hub of Northeast and North China. Indeed it is because of its important topography that all dynasties took great pains to develop the place, turning it into one of the world's largest cities and one of the best richly endowed with places of historical interest.

Beijing boasts the world's largest, well-preserved imperial palace — the Palace Museum; beautiful, magnificent imperial parks such as the Summer Palace and Beihai Park; huge, well-designed temples like the Temple of Heaven; the huge 5,000-kilometer-long military project of the Great Wall; the superbly-constructed necropolis of the Ming Tombs — anywhere you go in Beijing, whether under ancient pine and cypress trees, on the banks of the lakes and rivers or into the green hills and mountains, you can find historical sites and scenic spots quite beguiling.

Bejing is an excellent place for tourists. Tens of millions of visitors come to Beijing every year. In addition to enjoying the captivating beauty of the ancient yet modern city, they would appreciate an album to keep their memory of it fresh or to give to friends as a souvenir to let them share what they have seen in Beijing.

For them we have compiled this album. But Beijing's historical sites and scenic spots are too numerous for us to have included all of them. What you see here is but an epitome, which we hope will serve as a guide for you and your friends.

Vorwort

Beijing, die Hauptstadt der Volksrepublik China, ist eine weltbekannte Kulturstadt mit reicher Geschichte.

Vor dreitausend Jahren war Beijing ein strategisch wichtiges Städtchen namens Ji in Nordchina. In der Frühlings- und Herbstperiode und der Zeit der Streitenden Reiche (770-221 v. Chr.) war es die Hauptstadt des Staates Yan. In der ersten Hälfte des zehnten Jahrhunderts bestimmte die Liao-Dynastie (907-1125) es zu ihrer zweiten Hauptstadt und benannte es Nanjing (Südliche Hauptstadt) alias Yanjing. Mitte des zwölften Jahrhunderts errichtete die Jin-Dynastie (1115-1234) ihre Hauptstadt in Yanjing und änderte den Namen auf Zhongdu (Zentrale Hauptstadt), wo auch viele nachfolgende Dynastien ihre Hauptstadt hatten. Die Yuan-Dynastie (1271-1368) legte für Zhongdu die Bezeichnung Dadu (Große Hauptstadt) fest, bis 1403 Zhu Di, der vierte Sohn von Zhu Yuanzhang, dem Gründer der Ming-Dynastie (1368-1644), zum dritten Ming-Kaiser wurde und den Kaiserhof von Nanjing hierher verlegte. Die Stadt hieß nun Beijing (Nördliche Hauptstadt). Am 1.Oktober 1949 wurde die Volksrepublik China ins Leben gerufen, und Beijing ist zu ihrer Hauptstadt und zum Zentrum für Politik, Wirtschaft, Verkehr, Wissenschaft und Kultur in China geworden.

Beijing liegt am nördlichen Rand der ausgedehnten Nordchinesischen Ebene. Nordwestlich ist die Stadt von Bergen und südöstlich von Ebenen umgeben. Ihre geographische Lage machte sie in den vergangenen Dynastien zu einer strategisch wichtigen Stelle, die man umkämpfen mußte, und seit moderner Zeit ist sie ein Verkehrsknoten zwischen Nordost- und Nordchina. Eben wegen ihrer geographisch wichtigen Lage gaben sich alle Dynastien größte Mühe, die Gegend zu entwickeln, so daß Beijing eine der Metropolen der Welt mit zahlreichen Kulturdenkmälern geworden war.

Beijing besitzt den größten und am besten erhaltenen Kaiserpalast der Welt — die Verbotene Stadt. Es hat viele attraktive kaiserliche Gärten wie den Sommerpalast und den Beihai-Park; riesengroße und vortrefflich gestaltete Tempelanlagen wie den Himmelstempel; eine fünftausend Kilometer lange militärische Verteidigungsanlage — die Große Mauer — und eine ins Detail geplante Nekropole — die Ming-Gräber. Wo man auch hinkommt, kann man in Beijing, ob unter alten Kiefern und Zypressen, am Ufer der Seen und Flüsse oder in grünen Hügeln und Bergen, auf anziehende historische Ruinen oder Sehenswürdigkeiten stoßen.

Beijing ist ein faszinierendes Reiseziel. Jedes Jahr strömmen zahllose Besucher nach Beijing. Viele möchten ihre Eindrücke bewahren oder sie an Freunde vermitteln. Zu diesem Zweck haben wir den vorliegenden Band zusammengestellt. Beijing ist zu reich an Kulturdenkmälern und Sehenswürdigkeiten, so daß alles nicht in einen Bildband aufgenommen werden kann. Wir hoffen, daß wir Ihnen auch mit diesem sorgfältig ausgewählten Überblick Freude bereiten und Interesse erregen.

Avant-propos

Beijing, la capitale de la République populaire de Chine, est l'une des villes chargées d'histoire et de culture les plus célèbres au monde.

Il y a plus de 3 000 ans, Beijing, alors appelé Ji, était un bourg stratégique en Chine du Nord. A l'époque des Printemps et Automnes(770-476 av. J.-C.) et à celle des Royaumes combattants (475-221 av. J.-C.), Ji fut la capitale du Royaume de Yan. Au cours de la première moitié du Xe siècle, elle devint la capitale secondaire de la dynastie des Liao (907-1125), et reçut le nom de Nanjing (Capitale du Sud) ou Yanjing (Capitale de Yan). Au milieu du XIIe siècle, la dynastie des Jin (1115-1234) y fonda sa capitale et lui donna le nom de Zhongdu (Capitale du milieu). La ville de Beijing devint, dès lors, la capitale des dynasties suivantes. Les Yuan (1271-1368) rebaptisèrent Zhongdu Dadu — la Grande Capitale. En 1403, Zhu Di, quatrième fils de Zhu Yuanzhang, fondateur de la dynastie des Ming (1368-1644), transféra sa capitale de l'actuelle ville de Nanjing à Dadu et lui donna son nom actuel Beijing (Capitale du Nord). Le premier octobre 1949, fut fondée la République populaire de Chine et Beijing devint la capitale, le centre politique, économique, scientifique et culturel et le nœud de communications de la Chine nouvelle.

La ville de Beijing est entourée de montagnes au nord et à l'ouest et s'ouvre vers la Plaine de la Chine du Nord au sud et à l'est. Cette situation géographique a fait d'elle, depuis l'antiquité, une position stratégique et un nœud de communications entre la Chine du Nord et la Chine du Nord-Est. La construction de nombreux édifices sous les différentes dynasties a fait de Beijing une des villes les plus grandes et les plus riches en vestiges historiques du monde.

Vous pouvez y admirer la Cité interdite, le Palais impérial le plus grand et le mieux conservé du monde; le Palais d'Eté et le parc Beihai, jardins impériaux aux paysages pittoresques et aux constructions splendides; le Temple du Ciel, édifice imposant et d'une harmonie parfaite; la Grande Muraille, gigantesque ouvrage militaire qui s'étend sur une longueur de dx mille *li;* les Treize Tombeaux des Ming, nécropoles impériales rigoureusement disposées, etc. Vous trouverez partout, sous les pins et cyprès verdoyants, au bord des lacs ou rivières, ou sur les versants des collines, des sites historiques ou naturels qui vous captiveront et vous eront rêver.

Chaque année, des dizaines de millions de touristes venus de tous les coins du monde admirent les splendeurs de Beijing, et veulent en garder les images en mémoire. Pour répondre à ce désir, nous avons édité cet album intitulé *Beijing et ses merveilles* afin de présenter quelques-uns des sites historiques ou pittoresques de Beijing. Nous serons ravis si cet album peut vous être utile ou vous faire plaisir.

Tian'anmen
Das Tian'anmen-Tor
La porte Tian'anmen

The front gate to the royal palaces during the Ming Dynasty and Qing Dynasty, the center of the city of Beijing and the symbol of New China.

It was built in 1417 or the 15th year of the reign of Emperor Yong Le of the Ming Dynasty, called the Gate of Heavenly Succession. It was reconstructed in 1651 or the 8th year of the reign of Emperor Shun Zhi of Qing Dynasty and renamed Tian'anmen after the reconstruction. The original height of the rostrum is 33.7 meters. With its double-eaved roof upturning and its carved beams and painted rafters, with five exquisitely carved white-marble bridges straddling across the Golden Water Stream flowing down below the rostrum, it is so elegantly picturesque. The wonderful coordination between the two pairs of robust stone lions and two colossal, graceful and ornamentally carved columns in front of the rostrum makes Tian'anmen a perfect architectural masterpiece. It attracts every year a great number of Chinese and foreign tourists with its majestic appearance and long history.

Das Tian'anmen (Tor des Himmlischen Friedens) mit einer Höhe von 33,7 Metern ist das Haupttor des Kaiserpalastes. Es wurde 1417, zur Zeit der Ming-Dynastie, errichtet. Damals hieß es „Chengtianmen" (Tor der Stütze des Himmels). 1651, während der Regierungsperiode Shunzhi der Qing-Dynastie (1644-1911), wurde umgebaut und in Tian'anmen umbenannt.

Der obere Teil des Tors ist ein Holzbau mit roten Säulen und einem Doppeldach aus gelb glasierten Ziegeln. Vor dem Tor ist der „Fluß". Über den Fluß spannen die fünf Brücken aus weißem Marmor. Sie heißen die „Brücken des Goldwasser-Flusses". Vor dem Tian'anmen-Tor stehen zwei dekorative Marmorsäulen, „Huabiao" genannt, und vor dem Eingang des Tors und vor den Brücken befinden sich jeweils zwei steinerne Löwen.

C'était la porte principale du Palais impérial sous les Ming et les Qing. Située au cœur de la ville, la porte Tian'anmen est le symbole de la Chine nouvelle.

Construite en 1417 sous les Ming, c'était alors la porte Chengtianmen. En 1651 sous les Qing, elle fut reconstruite et reçut son nom actuel. Haute de 33,7 m, elle est surmontée d'une double toiture aux coins relevés et soutenue par des colonnes sculptées et des poutres peintes; la douve (Rivière aux Eaux d'or) qu'enjambent cinq ponts de marbre blanc finement sculptés coule à ses pieds; devant la porte, se dressent deux lions de pierre à l'air imposant et deux colonnes ornementales; tout cela fait de la porte Tian'anmen un ensemble architectural achevé. Cette porte ancienne et majestueuse attire chaque année de nombreux visiteurs chinois et étrangers.

Rostrum of Tian'anmen
Der Torturm des Tian'anmen
Le pavillon de la porte Tian'anmen

Tian'anmen Square is the largest of its kind in the world. It is large enough to accommodate half a million people at the same time. On the northern side stands Tian'anmen. At the center of the square is the Monument to the People's Heroes. The Mao Zedong Memorial Hall and the Zhengyangmen (popularly known as Qianmen [Front Gate]) are located on the southern side of the square. On the western side is the Great Hall of the People and on the eastern side the Museum of Chinese History and the Museum of the Chinese Revolution.

Der Tian'anmen-Platz befindet sich in der Stadtmitte Beijings, hat eine Fläche von 50 ha und dient als Besichtigungs- und Versammlungsort. Er kann über 500 000 Menschen aufnehmen. An der Nordseite des Platzes befindet sich das Tian'anmen-Tor, an der Südseite davon die Mao Zedong-Gedenkhalle und das Qianmen (vorderes

Tor), an der Westseite das Gebäude des Nationalen Volkskongresses und an der Ostseite die Museen für die Chinesische Geschichte und die Chinesische Revolution. Mitten auf dem Platz steht das Denkmal der Helden des Volkes.

La place Tian'anmen. C'est la plus grande place du monde et peut contenir 500 000 personnes. Au nord, c'est la porte Tian'anmen; au milieu, se dresse le Monument aux Héros du Peuple; au sud, se trouvent le Mémorial du président Mao Zedong et la porte Zhengyangmen (ou porte Qianmen); à l'ouest, c'est le Palais de l'Assemblée populaire; à l'est, le Musée d'Histoire de Chine et le Musée de la Révolution chinoise.

Night view of Tian'anmen

Das Tian'anmen-Tor bei Nacht

Vue nocturne de la porte Tian'anmen.

Carved ornamental columns

Dekorative Marmorsäule

Colonne ornementale.

Festive scene at Tian'anmen Square

Der Torturm des Tian'anmen am Festtag

La porte Tian'anmen en fête.

Built in 1959, the Museum of Chinese History and the Museum of Chinese Revolution are among the 10 great buildings built as gifts to the 10th anniversary of the founding of the People's Republic of China.

Das Gebäude der Museen für die Chinesische Geschichte und die Chinesische Revolution, 1959 erbaut.

Le Musée d'Histoire de Chine et le Musée de la Révolution chinoise font partie des dix grands édifices de Beijing, construits en 1959, pour célébrer le 10ᵉ anniversaire de la fondation de la République populaire de Chine.

Palace Museum
Der Kaiserpalast
Le Palais impérial

The Palace Museum was formerly called the Forbidden City. The construction began in 1406 or the 4th year of the reign of Emperor Yong Le, the third Ming Dynasty emperor, and was completed in 1420 or the reign of the 18th year of Emperor Yong Le. The Palace Museum was the court palaces for the Ming Dynasty and Qing Dynasty. It covers an area of 720,000 square meters. It contains over 9,000 rooms, and is surrounded by a moat 52 meters wide. The palace wall is 10 meters high and 3,000 meters long. At its four corners are beautifully styled watchtowers. The architectural setting of the Palace Museum is divided into two sections, the Front Court and Inner Palace. The Front Court includes the Hall of Supreme Harmony (Taihedian), the Hall of Perfect Harmony (Zhonghedian) and the Hall of Preserving Harmony (Baohedian). On the eastern and western sides of the Front Court are the Hall of Literary Glory and the Hall of Military Excellence. The Front Court was predominantly the place where the emperor conducted important state affairs, met with foreign ambassadors and envoys and held consultations with ministers; the Inner Palace is composed of the Hall of Heavenly Purity (Qianqinggong), the Hall of Union (Jiaotaidian), the Palace of Earthly Tranquility (Kunninggong). The Inner Palace was the place where the emperor conducted day-to-day government affairs and where the queen and princes lived. It lasted for more than 570 years and went through 24 emperors.

The architecture of the Palace Museum is majestic and is the essence of the classical Chinese art of architecture. It is also the largest existing classical architectural complex preserved intact. In 1987, UNESCO listed the Palace Museum as one of the Cultural Legacies of the World.

Der Kaiserpalast mit einer Gesamtfläche von 720 000 m², auch Zijincheng (die Purpurne Verbotene Stadt) genannt, wurde vom 4. bis zum 18. Jahr der Regierungsperiode Yonglo (1406-1420) der Ming-Dynastie erbaut. Die Kaiser der Ming- und der Qing-Dynastie arbeiteten und lebten hier. Auf dem Gelände des Kaiserpalastes befinden sich insgesamt 9999 Räume. Der Palast ist in drei Teile untergliedert: Waichao (Außenhof), Neiting (Innenhof) und der Kaiserliche Garten. Die Hauptbauwerke im Außenhof, wo die Kaiser ihre Minister in Audienz empfingen und verschiedene Zeremonien stattfanden, sind die „Drei Großen Hallen" — die Taihedian (Halle der Höchsten Harmonie), die Zhonghedian (Halle der Vollkommenen Harmonie) und die Baohedian (Halle zur Erhaltung der Harmonie). Die Innenhof, die Wohngemächer der Kaiser, Kaiserinnen und Konkubinen, bestehen hauptsächlich aus dem Qianqinggong (Palast der Himmlischen Reinheit), der Jiaotaidian (Halle der Berührung von Himmel und Erde) und dem Kunninggong (Palast der Irdischen Ruhe). 1987 wurde der Kaiserpalast in die Liste des Weltkultur- und Naturerbes" der UNESCO aufgenommen.

Le Palais impérial, appelé autrefois Cité interdite, a été la résidence des empereurs des dynasties des Ming et des Qing. Construit entre 1406 et 1420, le Palais impérial couvre une superficie de 720 000 m² et comporte plus de 9000 pièces. Il est entouré par une enceinte de 10 m de haut et de 3 000 m de long, et une douve de 52 m de large. Quatre tours d'angle se dressent aux quatre coins de l'enceinte. Le Palais impérial est divisé en deux parties: la cour extérieure et la cour intérieure. La Salle de l'Harmonie suprême (Taihedian), la Salle de l'Harmonie parfaite (Zhonghedian) et la Salle de l'Harmonie préservée (Baohedian), avec le Palais de la Culture (Wenhuadian) à l'est et la Salle des Prouesses militaires (Wuyingdian) à l'ouest, constituent la partie principale de la cour extérieure, où l'empereur exerçait son pouvoir et présidait les cérémonies solennelles. Le Palais de la Pureté céleste (Qianqinggong), la Salle de l'Union (Jiaotaidian) et le Palais de la Tranquillité terrestre (Kunninggong), avec les six palais de l'est et les six palais de l'ouest, forment la partie principale de la cour intérieure, où l'empereur réglait les affaires de l'Etat et se reposait, et où vivaient les impératrices, les concubines impériales et les princes. Ce fut la demeure de vingt-quatre empereurs de deux dynasties pendant plus de 570 ans.

Le Palais impérial est l'expression parfaite de la tradition et du style de l'architecture chinoise, et c'est aussi l'ensemble d'anciens palais le plus grand et le plus complet de Chine. Il a été classé, en 1987, par l'UNESCO, comme un des trésors du patrimoine culturel mondial.

Palace Museum
Der Kaiserpalast
Le Palais impérial.

Meridian Gate (Wumen).   This is the main entrance to the Palace Museum. The gate rises 8 meters high, and is flanked left and right by the Bell and Drum Pavilions. Built on the stone block are five buildings, generally known as the Five-Phoenix Tower.

Das Wumen-Tor   Das Wumen (Mittagstor), allgemein als Wufenglou (Turm der Fünf Phönixe) bekannt, ist der erste Eingang zum Kaiserpalast. Der untere Teil des Wumen besteht aus einer 10 m hohen zinnoberroten U-förmigen Mauer. An der rechten und der linken Seite stehen ein Glockenturm und ein Trommelturm.

La Porte du Méridien (Wumen) (en haut), entrée principale du Palais impérial, flanquée d'une tour de la cloche et d'une tour du tambour, d'une hauteur de 8 m, est surmontée de cinq pavillons d'où le nom de «Porte aux cinq pavillons».

A view of the Meridian Gate

Das Wumen von der Südseite aus

La Porte du Méridien vue du sud.

Watchtower viewed from the distance. At each corner of the Palace Museum wall is a three-storeyed watchtower exquisitely constructed of wood with triple eaves and 72 ridges. They are masterpieces of ancient Chinese architecture.

Wachturm in der Ferne. An den vier Ecken auf der Mauer der Verbotenen Stadt ruht je ein Wachturm in Holzkonstruktion. Diese Türme mit drei Dachvorsprüngen und 72 Dachfirsten sind Meisterwerke der altchinesischen Architektur.

Les tours d'angle aux quatre coins du Palais impérial sont des constructions en bois à triple toiture et à 72 faîtes. Elles sont des chefs-d'œuvre de l'architecture chinoise.

Watchtower

Wachturm (Nahaufnahme)

Une des tours d'angle.

Hall of Supreme Harmony

Die Halle der Höchsten Harmonie

La Salle de l'Harmonie suprême.

Interior of the Hall of Supreme Harmony

Innenansicht der Halle der Höchsten Harmonie

Vue intérieure de la Salle de l'Harmonie suprême.

Wall Decorated with Colored Glaze

Mauer mit glasierten Ziegeln

Mur vernissé.

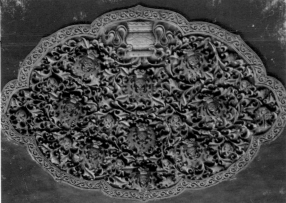

(*Right*) Gilded bronze statue of lion

Vergoldeter Löwe und Bronzelöwe *(rechts)*

Le lion doré et le lion de bronze (à droite).

Hall of Perfect Harmony.   This was where the emperor took a short rest while on his way to the Hall of Supreme Harmony, received people with the Ministry of Rites of the Cabinet, and read the memorials and message of congratulation to the throne.

Die Zhonghedian   (Halle der Vollkommenen Harmonie) war eine Stätte, in der sich der Kaiser ausruhte, bevor er sich zu feierlichen Zeremonien in die Halle der Höchsten Harmonie begab.

La Salle de l'Harmonie parfaite   était l'endroit où l'empereur se reposait avant d'aller présider des cérémonies dans la Salle de l'Harmonie suprême, ou recevait les respects présentés par ses ministres, ou encore lisait les rapports que ceux-ci lui soumettaient.

Interior of the Hall of Union

Innenansicht der Jiaotaidian (Halle der Berührung von Himmel und Erde)

Vue intérieure de la Salle de l'Union.

Imperial lane marble ramp. The marble ramp was carved out of a single block of green stone. It is 16.75 meters long, 3.07 meters wide, and 1.7 meters thick, and weighs about 250 tons. What was carved on the marble ramp was a dragon against a backdrop of clouds and sea waves, serving as a foil to the majesty of the imperial lane.

Der Kaiserweg aus geschnitztem Marmor   Ein großes Steinrelief „Drachen in den Wolken" befindet sich hinter der Halle zur Erhaltung der Harmonie und ist 16,75 m lang, 3,07 m breit, 1,7 m dick und 250 t schwer.

La voie impériale. Sculptée dans le marbre, cette dalle mesure 16,75 m de long, 3,07 m de large, 1,7 m d'épaisseur et pèse 250 tonnes. Elle est sculptée de dragons volant dans les nuages et les vagues. Tous ces motifs étaient destinés à rehausser la majesté du lieu.

Hall of Heavenly Purity.   During the Ming Dynasty and the early part of the Qing Dynasty, emperors lived and handled state affairs here. Emperor Yong Zheng of the Qing Dynasty read and commented on the memorials submitted to him by his ministers, gave audience to the ministers, and appointed officials here. In 1901 or the 27th year of the reign of Emperor Guang Xu, Empress Dowager Ci Xi on many occasions gave interviews to foreign ambassadors and envoys here.

Der Qianqinggong   (Palast der Himmlischen Reinheit) diente dem Kaiser als Schlafgemach. Mitunter erledigte er hier auch laufende Staatsgeschäfte und gab an Feiertagen seinen Ministern Bankette.

Le Palais de la Pureté céleste,   résidence de l'empereur et de l'impératrice, était aussi l'endroit où l'empereur réglait les affaires de l'Etat et recevait les émissaires étrangers. En 1901, l'impératrice douairière Cixi y reçut plusieurs fois des ambassadeurs étrangers.

Interior of the Hall of Heavenly Purity. "Open and Above Board" — the words written on the board hung high in the middle of the palace was the handwritting of Emperor Shun Zhi of the Qing Dynasty. He wrote these words to show what he did was honest, generous,open and upright.

Innenansicht von Qianqinggong   Auf der horizontalen Tafel im Palast stehen vier chinesische Schriftzeichen: „Guangming zhengda" (offen und ehrlich), in der Handschrift des Kaisers Shunzhi der Qing-Dynastie.

Vue intérieure du Palais de la Pureté céleste.   Le panneau horizontal à l'intérieur du Palais porte quatre caractères signifiant «franc et droit», calligraphiés par l'empereur Shunzhi des Qing.

Balustrades and steles.　　White marble steles and balustrades carved with dragon and phoenix patterns—they are all exquisite and magnificent.

Marmor-Balustraden

Balustrade et colonne. Elles sont en marbre blanc finement sculpté.

Carved red sandalwood cabinet in the palace. It is carved with the pattern of two dragons playing with a pearl.

Sandelholz-Schrank mit dem Muster „Zwei Drachen spielen mit einer Perle"

Meuble ciselé de santal rouge. Le motif sculpté sur le meuble représente deux dragons jouant avec une perle.

Exquisitely designed channel in the palace

Eingang

Des chemins ingénieusement aménagés dans la cour.

Thousand-Autumn Pavilion.   The Thousand-Autumn Pavilion and the Pavilion of Ten-Thousand Springs are two symmetrical buildings in the Imperial Garden. The structure of the pavilion and building is exquisite and diverse. It is made even more beautiful when coordinated with the rockeries, ancient cypresses and Taihu Rocks.

Der Pavillon aller Ewigkeit (Qianqiuting)   Der Pavillon befindet sich im Kaiserlichen Garten. Er steht dem Pavillon des Ewigen Frühlings (Wanchunting) gegenüber. Rings um die Pávillons gibt es künstliche Berge, alte Zypressen und Steinblöcke aus dem Taihu-See in der Provinz Jiangsu.

Le Pavillon des Mille Automnes (Qianqiuting). Le Pavillon des Mille Automnes et le Pavillon de la Longévité millénaire (Wanshouting) sont deux constructions symétriques dans le Jardin impérial. Les kiosques, les pavillons, les rocailles et les arbres font de ce jardin un lieu merveilleux.

Pavilion of Rain and Flowers

Yuhuage (Pavillon der Regenbluman)

Le Pavillon des Fleurs de Pluie (Yuhuage).

Wine cup on a winding stream.   Skirting the Floating Cups Pavilion in the Hall of Tranquil Longevity is an S-shape stream. When there were poets who visited the pavilion, they loved to sit and drink along the stream. Having had enough wine, they put the wine cup on the water and let it flow down the stream. In case there was a cup that stopped in front of a certain poet, he should drink an additional cup of wine and compose a poem.

Der Kanal für fließene Becher   Dieser kleine Kanal im Ningshougong-Garten verläuft in Windungen und Wendungen. Man ließ darauf Becher mit Wein oder Schnaps schwimmen, trank daraus und verfaßte dazu Gedichte. Daher rührt das geflügelte Wort: Auf gewundenem Wasser fließt der Becher.

Le Canal transportant les coupes   dans le jardin du Palais de la Tranquillité et de la Longévité (Ningshougong). Sur ce canal au parcours zigzaguant, on laissait flotter des coupes que les Invités attrapaient et l'on buvait en composant des vers.

Hill of Acumulated Excellences.　Every year at the Double Ninth Festival, the emperor and the queen walked up the hill to enjoy the sight.

Der Duixiushan (Hügel der Gesammelten Eleganz) Während des Chongyang-Festes (der 9. des 9. Monats nach dem chinesischen Kalender) begaben sich der Kaiser und seine Frauen und Konkubinen auf dem Duixiushan.

La Colline où s'amoncelle la Beauté (Duixiu-shan) était l'endroit où l'empereur et l'impératrice admiraient le paysage à l'occasion du 9e jour du 9e mois lunaire.

Zhenfei Well　Zhenfei was the beloved imperial concubine of Emperor Guang Xu of the Qing Dynasty. She supported Emperor Guang Xu in his political ideas. In 1900, Empress Dowager Ci Xi ordered a eunuch to push her into this well and drown her. That is why it has been called Zhenfei Well.

Der Zhenfei-Brunnen　Zhenfei war die Lieblingskonkubine des Kaisers Guangxu der Qing-Dynastie. Sie unterstützte den Kaiser Guangxu bei der Reformbewegung von 1898 und wurde 1900 auf Befehl der Kaiserinwitwe Cixi in diesen Brunnen geworfen. Daher erhielt der Brunnen den Namen „Zhenfei-Brunnen".

Le puits de la favorite Zhenfei.　Zhenfei, favorite de l'empereur Guangxu, fut rejetée dans ce puits en 1900, sur l'ordre de l'impératrice douairière Cixi, d'où le nom du puits.

Beihai Park
Der Beihai-Park
Le parc Beihai

Beihai Park, located to the northwest of the Palace Museum, covers an area of more than 700,000 square meters and is one of the major tourist spots in Beijing. It is also the most ancient and most splendid extant imperial garden outside the Palace Museum. In the early 10th century, rulers of the Liao Dynasty built a pleasure ground here. When Jin overthrew Liao, the capital city was renamed Zhongdu(Central Capital). In the 13th century, the Yuan rulers named the city Dadu (Great Capital), with Qionghua (Jade Flowery) Island and North Lake as its center. Qionghua Island was piled up with the sludge scooped up from the bottom of the lake. Yuan Emperor Kublai Khan gave audience to Italian traveler Marco Polo at Qionghua Island. Five-Dragon Pavilion was built on the northern bank of Taiye (Heavenly Water) Lake. In 1651 or the 8th year of the reign of Emperor Shun Zhi, White Dagoba was built on the ruins of the Moon Palace. This was the inner palaces in both the Ming and the Qing Dynasties. The White Dagoba is the highest height of Beihai, where visitors may enjoy the panoramic view of Beihai.

The Round City on the western side of the Southern Gate of the Beihai Park is 5 meters high, and covers an area of about 4,500 square meters. It was once a part of the imperial garden. In the city are the ancient pines and cypresses tastefully laid out. The main buildings in the Round City include the Hall to Receive the Light and the Jade Jar Pavilion.

Der Beihai-Park (Nordsee-Park) befindet sich nordwestlich des Kaiserpalastes und nimmt eine Fläche von 700 000 m² ein. Schon im 10. Jahrhundert wurde hier unter der Liao-Dynastie die kaierliche Sommerresidentz Yaoyu (Palast auf der Jade-Insel) erbaut. Während der Jin-Dynastie entstanden im Bereich des heutigen Nordsees die Qionghuadao (Insel der Erlesenen Jade) und der Guanghangong (Mondpalast). Unter der Yuan-Dynastie wurden die Anlagen auf der Insel dreimal renoviert und ausgebaut. Unter der Ming-Dynastie wurden hier Bau- und Renovierungsarbeiten ausgeführt. Die Fünf-Drachen-Lauben und die Neun-Drachen-Mauer, die am nördichen Ufer des Beihai-Sees liegen, sowie viele Türme, Pavillons und andere Bauten auf der Runden Stadt stammen aus der Ming-Zelt. Aber erst in der Qing-Zeit wurde der Beihai Park in großem Maßstab ausgebaut. 1651 wurde an der Stelle, wo der Guanhangong eingestürzt war, die Weiße Pagode im tibetischen Stil erbaut. Die Qionghuadao ist das Herz des Beihai-Parks. Darauf erhebt sich inmitten von Bäumen die Weiße Pagode.

Vor dem Südtor des Beihai-Parks zieht sich eine 5 m hohe ringförmige Mauer entlang. Hier liegt die Runden Stadt. Während der Jin-Dynastie im 12. Jahrhundert wurde der Beihai-Park ausgehoben und mit dem dabei gewonnenen Erdreich der Hügel für die 4500 m² große Runde Stadt aufgeschüttet. Das Hauptgebäude der Runden Stadt ist die Chengguandian (Halle der Sonnenstrahlenaufnahme) und der Yuwengting (Pavillon des Nephrit-Gefässes).

Le parc Beihai, d'une superficie de 700 000 m², se trouve au nord-ouest du Palais impérial. C'est un des principaux sites touristiques de la ville. Dès le Xe siècle, les Liao commencèrent à y construire des palais. Les Jin qui succédèrent aux Liao y établirent leur capitale Zhongdu. Au XIIIe siècle, les Yuan construisirent la cité de Dadu autour de l'île Qionghua, formée avec la terre rejetée au moment du creusement du lac. Marco Polo, célèbre voyageur italien y a été reçu par Koubilaï Khan, empereur des Yuan. Sous les Ming, on bâtit les Cinq Pavillons-Dragons sur la rive nord de l'étang Taiye. En 1651, sous les Qing, on érigea à l'emplacement du palais Guanghan, le Dagoba blanc, point culminant et symbole du parc Beihai, d'où les visiteurs peuvent avoir une vue d'ensemble sur le parc. Le parc Beihai était un jardin impérial sous les Ming et les Qing.

La Citadelle ronde se trouve du côté ouest de l'entrée sud du parc Beihai. D'une hauteur de 5 m et d'une superficie de 4 500 m², elle faisait partie du jardin impérial. La Citadelle ronde comprend un jardin tranquille où poussent des pins et des cyprès séculaires, ainsi que deux constructions principales: la Salle de la Lumière (Chengguangdian) et le Kiosque du Vase de jade noir (Yuwengting).

Beihai Park
Beihai Park
Le parc Beihai

(*Left*) White Dagoba. The White Dagoba was built in 1651 or the 8th year of the reign of Emperor Shun Zhi. In 1679 and 1731, the White Dagoba suffered from two devastatig earthquakes and were reconstructed. The White Dagoba stands 35.9 meters high.

Die Weiße Pagode *(links)* Die Weise Pagode mit einer Höhe von 35,9 Metern erhebt sich auf der Qionghua-Insel. Sie wurde im 8. Jahr der Regierungsperiode Shunzhi der Qing-Dynastie (1651) erbaut. 1679 und 1731 wurde sie bei einem Erdbeben zerstört und später wiederhergestellt.

Le Dagoba blanc *(à gauche)*. Construit en 1651 sous les Qing, il se dresse sur un socle de briques. Il fut détruit en 1679 et en 1731 par un tremblement de terre, puis fut restauré à plusieurs reprises. D'une hauteur de 35,9 m, le Dagoba blanc est le symbole du parc Beihai.

(*Right*) Lotus Flowers in Full Blossom at Yong'an (Eternal Peace)Bridge. Yong'an Bridge is sometimes called Duiyun (Gathering Clouds) and Jicui (Collecting Jadeite) Bridge. The bridge derives its name from the two identical archways (both 4-pillared and 3-storeyed) standing respectively on the northern side (called Duiyun Archway) and southern side (called Jicui Archway) of the bridge. The beautiful and full-blossomed lotus flower and the White Dagoba in the background make the Duiyun and Jicui Bridge even more conspicuous.

Die Yong'an-Brücke *(rechts)* Die Brücke wurde auch als Duiyun Jicui-Brücke bezeichnet. An der Nord- und Südseite der Brücke steht je ein Ehrenbogen aus Holz. Der eine heißt Duiyun, der andere Jicui. Daher bekam die Brücke den Namen.

Les nénuphars épanouis au Pont de la Paix éternelle (Yong'anqiao) *(en bas)*. Le pont s'appelle aussi le Pont où s'accumulent les nuages et la verdure. Son nom est dû aux mots «jicui» (la verdure accumulée) et «duiyun» (les nuages accumulés) inscrits sur deux portiques ornementaux en bois, situés au sud et au nord. C'est entre les nénuphars épanouis et le Dagoba blanc que le pont apparaît dans toute sa beauté.

Shanyin Hall and White Dagoba

Die Halle der Herzensgüte (Shanyindian) und die Weiße Pagode

La salle Sanyin et la pagode Blanche.

Figures of Buddha on the wall of the Hall of Good Cause

Buddhafiguren als Mauerdekoration der Shanyindian

Effigies de bouddhas au mur de la Salle de la Bienfaisance (Shanyindian).

Chamber of Heart Easing.   The chamber is located on the northern bank of Beihai Lake. It is also called "The Garden Within a Garden". Taihu Rocks in the chamber are exquisitely carved. The pavilion, hall, arch bridge, winding paths and circular corridors combine to make every step a scenery. The surrounding is quite tastefully laid out and quiet.

Der Jingxinzhai-Garten   befindet sich am Nordufer des Nordsees. Er wurde auch als Garten innerhalb des Gartens bezeichnet. Im Garten sind Pavillons, Gartenhäuschen, Wandelgänge und Bogenbrücken zu sehen.

Le Pavillon de la Tranquillité de l'Esprit (Jingxinzhai). Situé sur la rive nord du lac Beihai, c'est un jardin au sein du parc. Les rocailles, les kiosques, les belvédères, les ponts, les sentiers sinueux et les galeries forment un jardin agréable dans un cadre tranquille.

Spring Shade on the Jade Flowery Isle. This is one of the Eight Celebrated Scenic Spots of Yanjing. East of the White Dagoba is a stone tablet with the powerful and vigorous characters written by Emperor Qian Long.

Der Chunyin-Gedenkstein gehört zu den „Acht Landschaften von Yanjing". Er befindet sich östlich der Weißen Pagode. Die Inschrift „Qiongdaochunyin" ist die Handschrift des Kaisers Qianlong der Qing-Dynastie.

Les quatre caractères «L'ombre printanière sur l'île Qionghua» que porte la stèle à l'est du Dagoba blanc furent calligraphiés par l'empereur Qianlong des Qing. Cet endroit est un des Huit Sites de Yanjing.

Bronze Celestial Dew-Collecting Platter.　Emperor Wudi of the Han Dynasty was said to have collected dew with this kind of platter to mix medicament to prolong the life of the Emperor and the Queen.

Tongxian Chenglupan, eine bronzene Statue, die im 18. Jahrhundert gegossen wurde. Die Statue hält einen Teller zur Sammlung des Taus. Der Legende nach ließ der Kaiser Wudi der Han-Dynastie mit diesem Teller Tau sammeln und dann Arznei mit diesem Tau bereiten. Damit wollten er und seine Frauen und Konkubinen ihr Leben verlängern.

L'Immortel recevant la rosée. Cette colonne ornementale fut érigée au XVIIIᵉ siècle. Selon la légende, avec la rosée recueillie, l'empereur Wudi des Han fit préparer un élixir de longévité.

(Left) Water-bordering Corridor.　This corridor is a 2-storeyed, 60-compartment, water-bordering corridor for strolling, circling round the whole Qionghua Island by the waist like a colored ribbon. When visitors are strolling along the corridor, they simply cannot take so many things of beauty all in.

Der Linshui-Wandelgang (links)　Der Wandelgang ist ein zweistöckiger Wandelgang am Ufer der Qionghua-dao-Insel.

La galerie longeant la rive du lac Beihai (à gauche). Cette galerie à deux étages et à 60 travées enserre l'île Qionghua comme un ruban multicolore. Le paysage environnant réjouit la vue des visiteurs qui s'y promènent.

Five-Dragon Pavilion.   Located in the northwestern part of the Beihai Park, the pavilion was built in 1602 or the 30th year of the reign of Emperor Wan Li of the Ming Dynasty. It is actually a combination of 5 pavilions bordering the water. Hence the name Five-Dragon Pavilion. It was where the emperor went fishing, enjoyed the moonlight and watched fireworks.

Die Fünf-Drachen-Pavillons   befinden sich im Nordwesten des Nordsees. Sie wurden im 30. Jahr der Regierungsperiode Wanli der Ming-Dynastie (1602) erbaut. Die Kaiser und Kaiserinnen angelten hier und beobachteten den Mond und Feuerwerke.

Les Cinq Pavillons-Dragons (Wulongting). Construits en 1602 sous les Ming, situés au nord-ouest du lac Beihai, ce sont des pavillons sur pilotis où l'empereur et l'impératrice venaient pêcher à la ligne, contempler la lune et admirer les feux d'artifice. Ces pavillons ont été restaurés plusieurs fois.

Round City. Located on the western side outside the southern gate of Beihai Park, the 5-meter-high city covers an area of 4,500 square meters. It was once an imperial garden known for its well-knit architecture.

Die Tuancheng (Runde Stadt) befindet sich westlich des Südtors des Beihai-Parks. Sie ist 4500 m² groß. Ihr Mauer ist 5 m hoch.

La Citadelle ronde (Tuancheng) se trouve du côté ouest de l'entrée sud du parc Beihai. D'une hauteur de 5 m et d'une superficie de 4 500 m², c'était un jardin impérial.

Chengguangdian (Hall for Receiving the Light). This is a square hall within the Round City. It has a double-eaved roof in an unique style.

Chengguangdian (Halle der Sonnenstrahlenaufnahme). Als Hauptbauwerk der Runden Stadt hat diese rechteckige Halle ein Doppeldach und ist durch einen eigenartigen Stil geprägt.

La Salle de la Lumière (Cheng Guang Dian), principal édifice de la Citadelle ronde, est une construction au style particulier.

Inner Scene of the Hall to Receive the Light. The jade statue of Buddha in the hall was carved out of a single lump of white jade, gracefully molded, with its lustre limpid and mellow. The Buddha's head and the *kasaya* were adorned with priceless rubies and emeralds.

Innenansicht der Chengguangdian In der Chengguangdian ist eine Buddha-Statue aus Jade zu sehen. Diese milchweiße und glänzende Statue ist reich mit Edelsteinen geschmückt.

Vue intérieure de la Salle de la Lumière. La salle abrite une statue de Bouddha de 1,5 m de haut, sculptée dans un bloc de jade blanc et sertie de pierres précieuses.

Lacebark pine

Weißkifer in Tuancheng

Pin à écorce blanche.

Nine-Dragon Screen.　　Erected with 424 pieces of colored glazed tiles on a white marble foundation, the screen is 25.86 meters wide, 6.65 meters high and 1.42 meters thick. It depicts nine lifelike dragons sporting with pearls with their robust claws against the backgroud of misty billowy waves.

　　Die Neun-Drachen-Mauer　　Die Mauer ist ganz aus 424 bunt glasierten Ziegeln zusammengesetzt. Sie ist 6,65 m hoch, 1,42 m dick und 25,86 m lang. Darauf sind neun sich in Wolken und Wellen windende Drachen dargestellt. Dieses hervorragende, fünfhundert Jahre alte Kulturdenkmal ist von fabelhafter, farbenfrischer und lebendiger Darstellung.

　　Le Mur aux Neuf Dragons, magnifique écran composé de 424 tuiles vernissées de sept couleurs, repose sur un socle de marbre blanc. Long de 25,86 m, haut de 6,65 m et d'une épaisseur de 1,42 m, ce mur représente neuf dragons jouant avec des boules aux milieu des vagues.

Jade Jar. Also known as "Vast Sea of Jade" of Dushan or Black Jade Wine Jar, it was made in the early Yuan Dyanasty. It is 493 cm in circumference, 70cm high and weighs about 3.5 tons. The jar was painstakingly carved out of a single piece of black jade. The whole body of the jar was covered with patterns of sea waves, pipefish, sea horse, seapig, sea deer and sea rhino. In 1745, Emperor Qian Long bought it at a high cost and preserved it in the Hall to Receive the Light. In the 14th year of the reign of Emperor Qian Long, the Jade Jar Pavilion was built.

Das Yuweng (Nephrit-Gefäß) Im Zentrum der Runden Stadt liegt ein Pavillon mit einem blauen Dach und weißen Säulen. Hier befindet sich ein 0,7 m hohes, 1,35 m breites, 1,82 m langes und 3,5 t schweres Becken. Es ist aus einem einzigen Block Nephrit gearbeitet. Außen ist es mit einem Basrelief, bestehend aus Fischen, Drachen und mythischen Meeresungeheuern, verziert, die sich in Wellen tummeln. Innen ist ein von Kaiser Qianlong gedichtetes Lied über dieses Gefäß eingraviert.

Le vase en jade noir datant des Yuan mesure 1,82 m de long, 1,35 m de large, 0,7 m de hauteur, et pèse 3,5 tonnes. Ce vase sculpté dans un bloc de jade noir, est orné de motifs en relief représentant des vagues, des dragons, des chevaux, des porcs, des cerfs et des rhinocéros. En 1745, l'empereur Gaozong des Qing acheta le vase à un prix très élevé pour le mettre dans la Salle de la Lumière. Plus tard, sous le règne de l'empereur Qianlong, un kiosque fut construit pour abriter le vase.

Summer Palace
Der Sommerpalast
Le Palais d'Eté

It was formerly the site of the Garden of Clear Ripples. Located in the northwestern outskirts of Beijing, it lies about 15 km from downtown Beijing and is China's largest extant royal garden. In 1750 or the 15th year of the reign of Emperor Qian Long of the Qing Dynasty, 140 tons of silver was earmarked for the celebration of the birthday of his mother Empress Dowager Xiao Shen. A lake and a hill piled up to make Wengshan Wanshoushan (Longevity Hill) and to make the Kunminghu was dug Lake. The construction work lasted 15 years. In 1860, the Anglo-French Allied Forces invaded Beijing and this palace was looted and destroyed. In 1888 or the 14th year of Emperor Guang Xu, Empress Dowager Ci Xi used funds allocated for the establishment of the Imperial Navy to rebuild this palace. The new palace was renamed Yiheyuan (the Summer Palace). In 1900, when the Eight-Power Allied Forces invaded Beijing, the Summer Palace fell into another disaster. In 1902, Empress Dowager Ci Xi ordered reconstruction of the Summer Palace in one year. In 1914, it was opened to the public. In 1924, it became a public park. The Summer Palace is composed of Wanshoushan Hill, Kunminghu Lake and palace temples. After 1949, constant maintenance and renovation were made, and the Summer Palace becomes a wonderful scenic spot for Chinese and foreign tourists. In December 1998, the Summer Palace was declared World's Cultural Legacy by UNESCO.

Der Sommerpalast (Yiheyuan) befindet sich im Nordwesten Beijings. Die Gesamtfläche beträgt 290 ha, davon entfallen drei Viertel auf den See. Der Sommerpalast ist die besterhaltene kaiserliche Gartenanlge in China und besteht hauptsächlich aus dem Wanshoushan (Berg der Langlebigkeit) und dem Kunming-See. Er wurde aufgeteilt in ein Viertel für die Erledigung der Staatsgeschäfte, ein Wohn- und ein Vergnügungsviertel.

Im 15. Jahr der Regierungsperiode Qianlong der Qing-Dynastie (1750) ließ Kaiser Qianlong zur Feier des 60. Geburtstages seiner Mutter mit der Anlage des Qingyiyuan (Garten des Reinen Wassers) beginnen. Der ursprüngliche Wengshan-Berg wurde in Wanshoushan-Berg und der ursprüngliche Westsee in Kunming-See umgetauft. Als der Qingyiyuan 1765 fertig war, waren 140 t Silber verbraucht. Als die alliierten Interventionstruppen Englands und Frankreichs 1860 in Beijing eindrangen, plünderten sie alle wertvollen Kulturgegenstände im Garten Qingyiyuan und zerstörten bzw. verbrannten fast alle prachtvollen Bauten. Im 14. Jahr der Regierungsperiode Guangxu (1888) ließ die Kaiserinwitwe Cixi den Qingyiyuan mit Geldern, die für den Ausbau der kaiserlichen Flotte bestimmt waren, wiederherstellen. Der Qingyiyuan wurde in Yiheyuan (Garten der Guten Erholung und Bescheidenheit) umgetauft, wie er auch heute noch heißt.

Im Jahr 1900, als die alliierten Interventionstruppen der acht Mächte in Beijing eindrangen und die Kaiserinwitwe Cixi mit Kaiser Guangxu in die westchinesische Stadt Xi'an floh, wurde der Sommerpalast noch einmal stark zerstört. Nach ihrer Rückkehr nach Beijing ließ die Kaiserinwitwe wiederum eine riesige Summe Silber aufbringen, um ihn noch einmal instand zu setzen. 1924 wurde der Sommerpalast als öffentlicher Park freigegeben.

1998 wurde der Sommerpalast in die „Liste des Weltkultur- und Naturerbes" der UNESCO aufgenommen.

Situé dans la banlieue nord-ouest, à 15 km de la ville de Beijing, le Palais d'Eté est le plus grand jardin impérial de Chine. En 1750, à l'occasion du 60e anniversaire de sa mère, l'empereur Qianlong dépensa 140 tonnes d'argent pour faire aménager ce jardin avec un lac et une colline. Les travaux durèrent 15 ans. En 1860, le jardin fut pillé et brûlé par les armées anglo-françaises. En 1888, l'impératrice douairière Cixi détourna le budget destiné à la marine impériale pour le restaurer. Le jardin dut rebaptisé le Palais d'Eté. En 1900, l'Armée coalisée des Huit Puissances envahit Beijing et mit à sac le Palais d'Eté. En 1902, l'impératrice douairière Cixi ordonna de restaurer une nouvelle fois le Palais d'Eté. Les travaux durèrent un an. En 1924, il fut ouvert au public. Le Palais d'Eté est constitué de la Colline de la Longévité millénaire (Wanshoushan), du lac Kunming, et de pavillons, palais, galeries, kiosques et ponts. Après la Libération en 1949, la Palais d'Eté prit un nouvel aspect grâce à des réhabilitations. Ce jardin est un site très connu aussi bien en Chine qu'à l'étranger. Depuis 1998, il est sur la liste des trésors du patrimoine culturel mondial désignés par l'UNESCO.

Summer Palace

Der Sommerpalast

Le Palais d'Eté

Summer Palace in spring

Der Sommerpalast im Frühling

Le Palais d'Eté au printemps.

(*Left*) Bin Feng Bridge. One of the six stone bridges on the West Dyke, this is an imitation of the Su Dyke (West Lake, Hangzhou) built in the reign of Qing Dynasty Emperor Qian Long. The name comes from the "State Song"of the *Book of Songs*.

Die Binfeng-Brücke *(links)* Sie ist eine der sechs Brücken am Westlichen Damm.

(*à gauche*) Le pont Bin-feng est un des six ponts de pierre de la digue de l'ouest, construit sous le règne de l'empereur Qianlong, selon le modèle de la digue Sudi du Lac de l'Ouest à Hangzhou.

Grand Theater.   Built in 1891 or the 17th year of the reign of Qing Dynasty Emperor Guang Xu, this 21-meter-high theater was the largest of its kind in China at that time. As there are courts that connect the three storeys of the stage, different performances can be held simultaneous. This theater was especially built for Empress Dowager Ci Xi and Emperor Guang Xu to watch performances.

Die Theaterbühne   Die 21 m hohe Theaterbühne im Deheyuan (Garten der Tudend und Harmonie) ist das größte Theater im Sommerpalast. Sie ist ein imposantes Gebäude mit einem mehrstufigen Dach, zinnoberroten Geländern und grünen Säulen mit Goldeinlegearbeiten. Sie wurde zur Feier des 60. Geburtstages der Kaiserinwitwe Cixi mit 700 000 Tael Silber gebaut und stand speziell Cixi zur Verfügung.

Le grand théâtre. Construit en 1891, c'est le plus grand théâtre ancien de Chine. D'une hauteur de 21 m, et construit sur trois étages, il était destiné aux distractions de l'impératrice douairière Cixi et de l'empereur Guangxu.

(*Lower left*) The interior of the Hall of Billowy Jade.   The main building in the Hall of Billowy Jade was built in 1750. After the Reform Movement of 1898 or the 24th year of Emperor Guang Xu, Emperor Guang Xu was imprisoned here by the Empress Dowager Ci Xi. This place was made inaccessible by brick walls on the north, east and west sides.

Innenansicht der Yulantang *(links unten)*   Die Yulantang-Halle wurde 1750 erbaut und ist heute noch im Originalzustand erhalten. In einer der Nebenhallen der Yulantang wurde Kaiser Guangxu auf Betreiben der Kaiserinwitwe Cixi gefangengehalten, nachdem die Reformbewegung von 1898 gescheitert war.

Vue intérieure du Palais des Vagues de Jade *(en bas à gauche)*. Les principales constructions de ce palais furent construites en 1750. Après le Mouvement réformiste de 1898, l'empereur Guangxu fut enfermé dans ce palais par l'impératrice douairière Cixi.

Long Corridor. This refers to the covered walkway which extends 728 meters from the Gate of Inviting the Moon in the east to the Ten-Foot Stone Pavilion in the west. It is one of the famous garden sceneries in China. On its beams are covered with 8,000-odd paintings of the picturesque West Lake in Hangzhou, human figures, hills and waters, flowers and birds. It is a rare treasure of the art of architecture.

Der Wandelgang   Der überdachte, 728 m lange Wandelgang verläuft am Nordufer des Kunming-Sees entlang von Ost nach West. Alle Deckenbalken sind mit geschichtlichen oder mythologischen Szenen sowie Landschaftsmotiven bunt bemalt. Es gibt über 8000 Bilder.

La Longue Galerie   s'étend sur une longueur de 728 m et constitue un des sites les plus importants du Palais d'Eté. Ses charpentes sont décorées de plus de 8 000 peintures représentant des paysages ou des scènes historiques et mythologiques.

Court of Picture-Like Scenery. An important building complex on the western slope of Wanshoushan (Longevity Hill). When strolling through them and looking far into the distance, visitors would feel as if they were enjoying a landscape painting. That is where the name comes from.

Huazhongyou (Wander in Bildern) ist ein wichtiger Baukomplex am westlichen Berghang des Wanshoushan.

Le Kiosque aux Peintures naturelles (Huazhongyou) s'élève sur le versant ouest de la Colline de la Longévité millénaire. Du kiosque, on embrasse une vue magnifique sur le lac.

Zhongxiangjie (Archway of Buddhist Incense). This is a magnificent Buddhist archway.

Zhongxiangjie (Torbogen des Buddhistischen Wohlgeruchs) Dieser prachtvolle buddhistische Torbogen weist ebenfalls einen eigenartigen Stil auf.

Le magnifique portique du Monde des Bouddhas (Zhong Xiang jie).

Back Hill in Autumn

Der hintere Abhang des
Wanshoushan im Herbst

La colline de derrière du
Palais d'Eté en automne.

(*Left*) Suzhou Street in winter

Die Suzhou-Straße im Schnee *(links)*

La rue marchande de Suzhou après la neige *(à gauche).*

Baoyunge (Precious Cloud Pavilion).   Popularly known as the "Bronze Pavilion", it was built in 1755 or the 20th year of the reign of Qing Dynasty Emperor Qian Long.The kiosk made entirely of bronze is 7.55 meters high and weighs about 207 tons. Within the kiosk there were statues of Buddha. In 1900, when the Eight-Power Allied Forces invaded Beijing, the statues of Buddha and the door and windows were looted to the ground. In 1993, the Star Foundation of the United States purchased from a French collector 10 pieces of the looted bronze doors and windows for US$ 515,000 and returned them to China. Now they were reinstalled to their original positions.

Der Pavillon der Wertvollen Wolken (Baoyunge)   Der 7,55 m hohe Baoyunge steht auf einem Sockel aus Marmor und sieht wie ein grünlicher Holzbau aus. In Wirklichkeit ist der ganze Pavillon aus Bronze und wiegt 207 t. 1900 wurden 10 Tür- und Fensterflügel sowie Buddhafiguren daraus von Eindringlingen der acht Mächte geraubt. 1993 hat eine US-amerikanische Stiftung für 515 000 US-Dollar diese Kulturgegenstände gekauft und sie China zurückgegeben.

Pavillon aux Nuages précieux (Baoyunge). Appelé aussi Pavillon de Bronze (Tongting), il fut construit en 1755 sous les Qing, mesure 7,55 m de haut, pèse 207 tonnes, et abrite des statues de Bouddha. Lors de l'agression par l'Armée coalisée des Huit Puissances en 1900, les statues de Bouddha, les portes et les fenêtres furent enlevées. En 1993, la Fondation américaine Star a racheté pour 515 000 dollars dix portes et fenêtres de bronze conservées en France et les a rendues à la Chine.

(*Left*) Portrait of Empress Dowager Ci Xi.   This painting was presented to her by the American-Dutch painter Hubert Vos in 1905. It is now displayed in the Hall for Treasures.

Porträt von Cixi   Es ist ein großes Ölgemälde, das Cixi in ihrem 71. Lebensjahr (1905) zeigt. Es ist ein Werk des holländischen Malers Hubert Vos.

Le portrait de l'impératrice douairière Cixi *(à gauche)*, réalisé en 1905 par le peintre américain d'origine hollandaise Hubert VOS, est conservé actuellement dans la Salle des Trésors.

Xiequyuan (Garden of Harmonious Interests).   It is known as the "Garden within a garden".In 1751, it was built in imitation of the Jichangyuan Garden (Pleasure Garden) in Wuxi, Jiangsu. It was renovated in 1811 and was destroyed later by the Eight-Power Allied Forces. It was rebuilt in the reign of Emperor Guang Xu and Empress Dowager Ci Xi made frequent visits to this garden for pleasure, enjoying the sight of swimming fish and angling.

Xiequyuan   (Garten der Geselligkeit), der auch als „Garten innerhalb des Gartens" bekannt ist, wurde 1751 nach dem Muster des Gartens der Ergötzung (Jichangyuan) auf dem Huishan-Berg nahe der Stadt Wuxi, Provinz Jiangsu, erbaut.

Jardin de l'Harmonie et de l'Intérêt (Xiequyuan).   Construit en 1751 d'après le style d'un jardin de Wuxi du Jiangsu et reconstruit en 1811, ce «jardin dans le jardin» fut détruit par l'Armée coalisée des Huit Puissances et restauré sous le règne de l'empereur Guangxu des Qing. L'impératrice douairière Cixi y venait souvent pour pêcher à la ligne.

Qingyanfang (Boat for Pure Banquets).   Also known as the Marble Boat, this 36-meter long boat was built in 1755. Rebuilt in 1893, it was carved out of large stone blocks.The double-decked cabin was of wooden structure, but was painted in marble veins. The cabin was decorated with stained glass windows. The marble boat was built to show that the rule of the Qing Dynasty was unshakable.

Qingyanfang   (Schiff der Friedlichen Ruhe) ist ein 36 m langes zweistöckiges Marmorschiff, das symbolieren sollte, daß die Qing-Dynastie fest wie Stein ist und nie untergeht.

Bateau pour les Banquets (Qingyanfang).   Appelé aussi Bateau de Marbre, il fut bâti en 1755 et reconstruit en 1893. Ce célèbre édifice mesure 36 m de long et est composé de gros blocs de pierre pour la fondation et de bois peint à motifs de marbre pour le pavillon. Les vitres sont multicolores. Cette construction symbolise la stabilité de l'empire Qing.

Spring Heralding Pavilion. Water-ringed, it is planted with many weeping willows on its perimeter. Willows are the first to bud to herald the coming of spring.

Der Pavillon der Frühlingsahnung (Zhichunting) ist von Wasser umgeben. Rings um den Pavillon wachsen üppige Weiden, deren Kätzchen früher als die der Weiden an anderen Orten aufspringen.

Le Kiosque de la Perception du Printemps (Zhichunting) est entouré de saules dont les premiers bourgeons annoncent l'arrivée du printemps.

Jade Belt Bridge. The bridge is the most famous among the six bridges on the West Dyke. The bridge itself, railing and steles are all carved out of white marbles and green stones, just like a belt of jade. When emperors and queens went to the Jade Spring Hill by boat, they must pass through this bridge.

Die Yudai-Brücke (Jadegürtel-Brücke) ist die bekannteste unter den sechs Brücken auf dem westlichen Damm. Während der Qing-Dynastie mußten Kaiser und Kaierinnen mit dem Schiff unter der Brücke hindurchfahren, wenn sie zum Yuquan-Berg (Jadequellen-Berg) wollen.

Le Pont de la Ceinture de Jade (Yudaiqiao), en marbre blanc, était le seul pont que devaient passer l'empereur et l'impératrice pour aller à la Colline de la Source de Jade en bateau.

The 17-Arch Bridge. This the longest stone bridge in the Summer Palace. It is 150 meters long, spanning across the East Dyke and South Lake Isle. It is just like a long rainbow sleeping on the waves. Its shape has the characteristics of the Lugou Bridge.

Die Siebzehn-Bogen-Brücke ist die längste Brücke im Sommerpalast, durch die die Nanhu-Insel mitten im Kunming-See und der Ostdamm des Sees miteinander verbunden sind.

Le Pont aux Dix-Sept Arches. Long de 150 m, c'est le plus grand pont de pierre du Palais d'Eté. Il relie, tel un arc-en-ciel, la digue est à l'île. Ce pont ressemble beaucoup au pont Marco Polo.

Bronze Ox. Sitting on the eastern bank of the Kunminghu Lake, it was cast in 1755 or the 20th year of Emperor Qian Long. On its back there cast an inscription of eighty Chinese seal characters — Gold Ox Inscription.It is said to be cast for the purpose of "flood-taming".

Der Bronzebüffel Der Bronzebüffel mit Inschriften befindet sich am Ostenufer des Kunming-Sees. Er wurde 1755 gegossen. Der Legende nach konnte er Hochwasser bezwingen.

Le buffle en bronze, coulé en 1755, se trouve sur la rive est du lac Kunming et porte sur son dos des inscriptions. Cette sculpture très expressive est aussi connue sous le nom de buffle d'or, censé dompter les inondations.

At the back of Wanshoushan (Longevity Hill) is a massive complex of buildings forming a Tibetan-style temple. It was devastated in wars. This is the restored temple.

Am hinteren Hang des Wanshoushan befindet sich eine Tempelanlage im tibetischen Stil. Sie wurde in kriegerischen Auseinandersetzungen schwer beschädigt. Unser Bild zeigt den restaurierten Tempel.

Un ensemble d'édifices au style tibétain sur le flanc nord de la Colline de la Longévité millénaire.

Yulantang (Hall of Magnolia)

Die Yulan-Halle

Le palais des Vagues de Jade.

Qingzhixiu Rock

Yadestein „Qingzhixiu"

Le jade Qingzhi.

Temple of Heaven
Der Himmelstempel
Le Temple du Ciel

It is the place where the emperors of the Ming and Qing Dynasties used to offer sacrifices to the Heaven and to pray for good harvest. It was built in 1420 or the 18th year of the reign of Emperor Yong Le of Ming Dynasty, called the Temple of Heaven and Earth. It was renamed the Temple of Heaven in 1534 or the 13th year of the reign of Emperor Jia Jing of Ming Dynasty. The Temple of Heaven is now the largest extant temple building complex of China. It covers an area of 2,700,000 square meters. In 1998, it was listed as one of the World's Cultural Legacies by the UNESCO.

The Temple of Heaven is enclosed by a double wall and is divided into the inner and outer temple. The southern wall is square and the northern round, symbolizing the heaven is round and the earth square. The main buildings are connected by a long flight of stone stairs, 360 meters long. The main buildings include Qiniandian (Hall of Prayer for Good Harvest), Huangqiongyu (Imperial Vault of Heaven), Huanqiutan (Circular Mound Altar) etc. The overall layout is exquisite and the art of architecture ingenious. It is really a rare treasure of art and cultural legacy in the world's history of architecture.

Der Himmelstempel (Tiantan) ist der Ort, wo die Kaiser der Ming- und Qing-Dynastie zum Himmel um eine reiche Ernte beteten. Er wurde im Jahre 1420 fertiggestellt. Tiantan ist heute der größte Tempelkomplex Chinas, nimmt eine Fläche von 2,7 Millionen Quadratmetern ein und wurde 1998 in die „Liste des Weltkultur- und Naturerbes" der UNESCO aufgenommen.

Der Tiantan ist von zwei Mauern — einer Innen- und einer Außenmauer — umgeben. Die Hauptbauwerke Qiniandian (Halle der Ernteopfer), Huangqiongyu (Halle des Himmelsgewölbes) und Huanqiutan (Himmelsalter) konzentrieren sich am Nord- und Südende einer 360 m langen Terrasse. Der gesamte Baukomplex weist eine ins Detail konzipierte Gestaltung und harmonische Farbgebung auf.

Sous les dynasties des Ming et des Qing, c'était l'endroit où les empereurs priaient pour les bonnes récoltes. Construit en 1420 sous le règne de l'empereur Yongle des Ming, c'était le «Temple du Ciel et de la Terre». En 1534 sous le règne de l'empereur Jiajing des Ming, il devint «Temple du Ciel». D'une superficie totale de 2,7 millions de mètres carrés, c'est aujourd'hui le plus grand groupe de constructions de sacrifice de Chine. En 1998, le Temple du Ciel a été classé parmi les trésors du patrimoine culturel mondial par l'UNESCO.

Le Temple du Ciel est entouré d'une double enceinte avec les murs sud droits et les murs nord en arc de cercle pour correspondre à l'idée d'une voûte céleste arrondie et d'une terre carrée. La Salle des prières pour les Bonnes Récoltes (Qiniandian), la Voûte céleste impériale (Huangqiongyu), l'Autel circulaire (Huanqiutan), et les autres constructions principales sont reliées par une chaussée de pierre de 360 m de long. Ce groupe de constructions constitue un ensemble architectural digne de figurer parmi l'héritage culturel de l'humanité.

(*Left*) Ancient Cypresses in the Temple of Heaven.   There are a large number of ancient cypresses in Tiantan or the Temple of Heaven. The growing age of the cypresses averages more than 600 years. They are evergreen and look a mass of branches and leaves round the year.

Alte Zypressen *(links)*   In Tiantan gedeihen viele Zypressen im Alter von mehr als 600 Jahren.

Vieux cyprès du Temple du Ciel *(à gauche)*. Le parc abrite nombre de cyprès verdoyants, vieux de plus de 600 ans.

Zhaigong (Abstinence Palace). This is the place where emperor came to offer sacrifices and commence fast. It is surrounded by high walls and the main hall is built with bricks and stones only, generally known as the Beamless Palace. Nine days before the ceremony was held, emperor go visit the Temple of Heaven and stay in this palace.

Zhaigong (Fastenpalast), auch als der „Balkenlose Palast" bezeichnet, wo die Kaiser ein Bad nahmen und drei Tage lang fasteten, bevor sie zum Himmel um eine reiche Ernte beteten.

Le Palais de l'Abstinence (Zhaigong). C'était l'endroit où l'empereur faisait abstinence avant la cérémonie de sacrifice. A l'intérieur d'un haut mur d'enceinte, se trouve la Salle sans Poutre, en briques et en pierre.

(*Upper*) Chengzhen Gate (Gate of Attaining Virtue). This gate is the main entrance to the Huangqiongyu and Huanqiutan.

Das Chengzhen-Tor *(oben)* ist der Eingang, der zu der Huangqiongyu und dem Huanqiutan führt.

La Porte de la Perfection et de la Fidélité (Chengzhenmen) *(en haut)*, qui donne l'accès à la Voûte céleste impériale et à l'Autel circulaire.

(*Lower*) The Temple of Heaven in spring peach flower in full blossom in spring, coordinated with the exquisite pavilions, make the visitors deeply feel the beauty of nature.

Tiantan im Frühling *(unten)* Die im Frühling in voller Blüte stehenden Pfirsichbäume und die Pavillons stellen ein schönes Bild dar.

Le Temple du Ciel au printemps *(en bas)*. Quand les pêchers sont en fleurs, le parc est vraiment un lieu merveilleux.

Jufutai (Terrace for Hanging Clothes). This was the place where the emperor rectified his clothes for the sacrifices.

Jufutai-Terrasse Dies ist der Platz, wo sich die Kaiser vor der Anbetung des Himmels umzogen.

La Terrasse pour l'Habillement (Jufutai). C'était l'endroit où l'empereur s'habillait avant la cérémonie.

(Right) Red Stairway Bridge. This is a white marble bridge connecting the Qiniandian and Huangqiongyu in the inner Temple of Heaven. It is 360 meters long, 28 meters wide and 2.5 meters high. The length of the bridge symbolizes the long distance between the Heaven and the Earth.

Danbiqiao (rechts) Die Brücke der Roten Palaststufen (Danbiqiao) aus weißem Marmor ist der Durchgang zur Qiniandian und Huangqiongyu. Sie ist 360 Meter lang, 28 Meter breit und 2,5 Meter hoch.

La Voie sacrée (Danbiqiao) (à droite). Long de 360 m, large de 28 m, et haut de 2,5 m, ce passage de marbre blanc relie la Salle des Prières pour les Bonnes Récoltes à la Voûte céleste impériale et symbolise le long trajet entre le ciel et la terre.

(*Left*) Qiniandian.   This is the place where the emperors of the Ming and Qing Dynasties prayed for good harvest. It is a huge round-shaped building, surmounted by a gilded spiral roof featuring triple-tiered eaves. Its structure is ingenious and its shape unique. It is of very high artistic value.

Qiniandian *(links)* In der Qiniandian (Halle der Ernteopfer) erflehten die Ming- und Qing-Kaiser jedes Jahr eine reiche Getreideernte. Die Halle ist eine runde Holzkonstruktion und weist einen einzigartigen architektonischen Stil auf.

La Salle des Prières pour les Bonnes Récoltes (Qiniandian) *(à gauche).* Réservée aux prières des empereurs des Ming et des Qing pour les bonnes récoltes, cette gigantesque construction circulaire à triple toiture est remarquable par sa forme particulière et sa grande valeur artistique.

Long Gallery.   Also known as the Seventy-two Connected Houses, this gallery was the only way for delivering sacrifices.

Der lange Korridos, auch als die „72-Verbundenen-Häuser" bekannt, war als Weg für den Transport der Opfergaben bestimmt.

La Longue Galerie,   appelée aussi «72 pièces reliées». C'était le passage nécessaire pour transporter les objets de sacrifice.

Exterior of Huangqiongyu

Die Halle des Himmelsgewölbes

La Voûte céleste impériale.

Exquisite glazed decorations on the roof of Huangqiongyu

Dachdekoration der Halle des Himmelsgewölbes

Ornements vernissés sur la Voûte céleste impériale.

Huangqiongyu (Circular Mound Altar). It is home to the memorial tablet of Huangqiutan. Due to the flatness and smoothness of the inner side of the wall, sound can be transmitted along the inner arc. That is why it is also called Echo Wall.

Huangqiongyu (Himmelsgewölbe)   Dort wurde die Gedenktafel des „Himmelsgottes" aufbewahrt. Die Innenseite der Mauer wird als „Echomauer" bezeichnet, weil sich hier der Schall auf optimale Weise fortpflanzt.

La Voûte céleste impériale (Huangqiongyu), destinée à abriter les tablettes pour le sacrifice. Le mur d'enceinte qui facilite la transmission des sons grâce à sa paroi intérieure lisse est aussi appelé Mur de l'Echo (Huiyinbi).

Huanqiutan (Circular Mound Altar).   Every year at the time of the winter solstice, the emperor came here to offer sacrifice to the Heaven. Also known as the Terrace for Offering Sacrifice to the Heaven, Huanqiutan was built in 1530 or the 9th year of the reign of Emperor Jia Jing of Ming Dynasty and underwent reconstruction in 1749. The surface of the altar was paved with mugwort-leaf-green stone and the balustrades and steles were carved out of white marble. Round-shaped and triple-tiered, Huanqiutan is surrounded by double low walls, the inner wall being round and the outer square, symbolizing that the Heaven is round and the Earth square. Exposed to wind and rain for more than 200 years, it remains intact and is one of the major scenic spots in the Temple of Heaven.

Huanqiutan (Himmelsaltar)   ist der Platz, wo der Kaiser jedes Jahr zur Wintersonnenwende dem Himmel opferte. Der Altar wurde im Jahre 1530 fertig gebaut und im Jahre 1749 ausgebaut. Seine Oberfläche ist mit Steinen belegt. Die Treppen und Geländer aus weißem Marmor sind fein bearbeitet. Der dreistöckige Huanqiutan ist kreisförmig.

L'Autel circulaire (Huanqiutan). Construit en 1530 sous le règne de l'empereur Jiajing des Ming et agrandi en 1749 sous les Qing, c'était l'endroit où l'empereur offrait des sacrifices au ciel, au moment du solstice d'hiver. L'autel circulaire à trois niveaux est dallé de pierres et entouré de balustrades de marbre. Deux murs d'enceinte bas, l'un circulaire à l'intérieur, et l'autre carré à l'extérieur, symbolisent la voûte céleste et la terre carrée. L'autel est bien conservé malgré 200 ans d'histoire et constitue l'un des sites les plus importants du Temple du Ciel.

North gate of Huanqiutan

Das Nordtor des Himmelsaltars

Entrée nord de l'Autel circulaire.

Qixingshi (Seven-Star Stones). They are believed to be meteors but are actually man-made objects symbolizing natural phenomena. It is also known as Zhenshi (Stoneweight).

Qixingshi (Sieben-Sterne-Steine) Es hieß früher, daß sie Meteoriten seien. In Wirklichkeit sind sie künstlich bearbeitet und symbolisieren Naturerscheinung.

Rochers à Sept Etoiles (Qixingshi). Ce sont des rochers artificiellement sculptés pour symboliser des phénomènes du ciel.

Nine-Dragon Cypress. The tree is so knotted that it seems entwined by nine dragons.

Jiulongbai (Zypresse der Neun Drachen) sieht so geknotet aus, als wäre sie von neun Drachen umwunden.

Cyprès aux neuf dragons.

Double-Ring Pavilion.　Two pavilions combined together, it is exquisitely designed and the shape extraordinary.

Der Shuanghuanting (Zwei-Ringe-Pavillon) besteht aus zwei nebeneinanderliegenden runden Lauben.

Pavillon double.

Grand View Garden
Daguanyuan
Le Jardin aux Spectacles grandioses

Skirted by a moat, Daguanyuan (Grand View Garden) in southwestern of Beijing was built in the 1980s. Its rockeries, ponds and buildings are all based on the distinguished classical Chinese novel *A Dream of Red Mansions* by Cao Xueqin of the Qing Dynasty, which describes the love story and tragic fate of Jia Baoyu, Lin Daiyu and Xue Baochai.

Daguanyuan reproduces the sights in the novel. A visit to the garden will strike a chord in the hearts of the visitors and make them reflect on the ancient events.

Daguanyuan (Garten der Großen Ansicht), der an der südöstlichen Ecke von Beijing liegt, wurde in den 80er Jahren angelegt. Seine Hügel, Teiche und Bauten basieren alle auf dem klassischen chinesischen Roman „Traum der Roten Kammer". Der Roman schildert anhand der Liebe und des tragischen Schicksals von Jia Baoyu, Lin Daiyu und Xue Baochai den Auf- und Untergang der chinesischen feudalen Aristokratie im 18. Jahrhundert. Ein Besuch des Gartens läßt einen an die alten Zeiten Chinas erinnern.

Construit au milieu des années 80 dans le sud-ouest de Beijing, le Jardin aux Spectacles grandioses (Daguanyuan) reproduit les scènes décrites par Cao Xueqin dans *Le Rêve dans le Pavillon rouge*. Ce célèbre roman classique chinois raconte une histoire d'amour tragique entre Jia Baoyu, Lin Daiyu et Xue Baochai, et reflète la décadence de la société féodale chinoise au XVIIIᵉ siècle.

Grand View Garden

Der Daguanyuan

Le Jardin aux Spectacles grandioses

House Reunion.   This is the temporary palace for the imperial consort Jia Yuanchun.

Villa des Familienbesuchs   Dieser Baukomplex war der vorläufige Palast für Jia Yuanchun, eine Nebenfrau des Kaisers.

La Villa pour le Retour (Xingqinbieshu). C'est la résidence de Jia Yuanchun, dame d'honneur de l'empereur, lorsqu'elle retourne chez elle pour voir ses parents.

Palace of Recalling Imperial Favor and Mindful of Duty.   This is the main building of the Grand View Garden, with a magnificently decorated interior that shows the majesty of the Imperial Consort.

Der Palast „Erinnerung an die Güte des Kaisers und Denken an die Pfticht" *(unten)* Dieser prachtvolle Palast ist das Hauptbauwerk der Villa des Familiebesuchs.

La Salle de la Reconnaissance et de la Loyauté (Gu'ensiyidian). C'est la construction principale de la Villa pour le Retour, dont l'intérieur est magnifiquement décoré.

Happy Red Court. This is where Jia Baoyu lives.

Der Glückliche Rote Hof Hier lebte Jia Baoyu, der Held des Romans „Traum der Roten Kammer".

La Cour du Rouge joyeux (Yihongyuan), résidence de Jia Baoyu, héros du roman.

Chamber of Happy Red and Delightful Green. This is Jia Baoyu's bedroom, with four beautiful wax-maids standing in it. This symbolizes mainly his unconventionality, his rebellious nature which leads him to befriend the lower-class people, and the affluence of a young noble.

Kammer des Glücklichen Rots und Fröhlichen Grüns Diese Kammer war das Schlafgemach von Jia Baoyu. In der Kammer stehen, in Wachs modelliert, vier Mädchen. Jia Baoyu hatte einen rebellischen Charakter, der ihn dazu führt, die feudale Ethik zu brechen und sich mit Menschen aus niedriger Klasse zu befreunden.

Le Rouge joyeux et le Vert Heureux (Yihongkuailü), chambre de Jia Baoyu. Les quatre belles servantes de cire représentent son caractère rebelle et la vie fastueuse qu'il mène.

Corridor of the Happy Red Court.   It is decorated with colored paintings covered by gold foils. When strolling in it, visitors would feel as if they were in a scroll.

Der Korridor des Glücklichen Roten Hofs   Dieser Korridor ist farbenprächtig dekoriert und gleicht einer Galerie.

La longue galerie peinte de la Cour du Rouge joyeux

有鳳來儀

Xiaoxiang Lodge.　This is the courtyard of Lin Daiyu, the main heroine of the novel. Her living quarters are decorated dominantly in pale green color to bring out her character — aloof, proud and grieved for living on others.

Das Xiaoxiang-Haus　Das Haus war die Unterkunft von Lin Daiyu, der Hauptheldin des Romans. Um ihren Charakter zu offenbaren, ist die Anlage blaßgrün gestrichen.

Le Studio de Xiaoxiang,　résidence de Lin Daiyu, une autre héroïne du roman. Cette construction vert clair traduit le chagrin et le marcissisme de cette jeune fille qui vit aux dépens des autres.

Alpinia Park.   This is the place where Xue Baochai, another heroine of the novel, lives. The grotesquely-shaped rocks embellishing the courtyard symbolize the serious and solemn nature of this girl from the nobility.

Der Garten des Duftenden Grases   Hier lebte Xue Baochai, eine andere Heldin des Romans. Die Felsen im Hof symbolieren das seriöse und ernste Wesen dieses Mädchens aus vornehmer Familie.

La Cour du Parfum (Hengwuyuan), résidence de Xue Baochai, héroïne du roman. Les rochers aux formes déchiquetées dans la cour représentent le caractère sérieux et strict de cette jeune fille et la richesse de sa famille.

Paddy-Sweet Cottage.   This is the place where Li Wan, Baoyu's sister-in-law, lives. Ringed by bamboo fences and thached cottages, with Jiuhuangzi (Wine shop sign: a piece of cloth hung in front of a wine shop to attract visitors) and fruit trees dotted among them, the paddy-sweet cottage is very idyllic.

Die Hütte des Reis-Duftes   Hier lebte Li Wan, die Schwägerin von Jia Bauyu.

Le Village au Parfum de Riz (Daoxiangcun), résidence de Li Wan, belle-sœur de Jia Baoyu. Les chaumières, les clôtures en bambou, les enseignes de bistrot, et les arbres fruitiers reproduisent un paysage champêtre.

Dripping Emerald Pavilion.　Construction of this lake pavilion is based on the story of Xue Baochai chasing a butterfly. Visitors can hear the sound of dripping water. The lake scene is very quiet and elegant.

Pavillon des Tropfenden Smaragdgrüns　Der Pavillon wurde in　Anlehnung an die Geschichte „Xue Baochai verfolgt einen Schmetterling" erbaut.

Le Kiosque vert émeraude (Dicuiting). Construit au milieu d'un lac, c'est l'endroit où Xue Baochai s'amuse avec des papillons.

Lotus Fragrance Anchorage.   Built close to a lake, the Lotus Fragrance Anchorage is a place for visitors to relax and enjoy fish swimming among the lotus and the reflections of the hanging willows on the lake.

Wasserpavillon des Lotos-Duftes   Vom Pavillon aus kann man die unter dem Lotos schwimmenden Fische und das Spiegelbild der Trauerweiden im Wasser bewundern.

Le Pavillon au Parfum de Lotus (Ouxiangxie) a été construit au bord de l'eau. Les visiteurs peuvent y admirer les saules pleureurs, les poissons et les fleurs de lotus.

Refreshing Fragrant Pavilion.   Surrounded by blossoming flowers and weeping willows, this lakeside pavilion is very refreshing.

Duftspendender Pavillon   Der am See gebaute Pavillon mit den Blumen und Bäumen rundherum ist ein schöner Erfrischungsort.

Le Kiosque du Parfum (Qinfangting), au bord de l'eau, où l'on peut sentir le parfum des saules pleureurs et des fleurs.

Great Wall
Die Große Mauer
La Grande Muraille

The Great Wall was listed as one of the World's Cultural Legacies in 1987 by the UNESCO. Today it measures about 6,700 km from Shanhaiguan Pass in Hebei Province to the Jiayuguan Pass in Gansu Province. Construction of the Great Wall began during the Warring States Period, right until 221 BC, spanning more than 200 years. Following China's unification under Qin Shihuang, the first emperor of the Qin Dynasty, in order to deter the harassing attacks from the Huns in the north, efforts were made to connect scattered segments into one huge rampart. It was afterward repaired and maintained right until the Ming Dynasty, undulating for thousands of kilometers. Many battlements, built at regular intervals all along the wall, were used as beacon towers.

The Badaling section of the Great Wall is the best preserved and the most integrated segment of the Great Wall. It rises and falls in concert with the ridges of the mountains. Its average height is 6.6m; width 6.5m at the base and 5.5m at the top. It is a crystalization of the wisdom on the part of the working people in the old times and also a symbol of Chinese ancient civilization. Now, an autobahn connecting Madian and Badaling was officially inaugurated on November 9,1998. It takes only one hour from downtown Beijing to the Badaling section of the Great Wall.

Die Große Mauer ist eine Verteidigungsanlage, mit deren Bau vor mehr als 2500 Jahren begonnen wurde. Damals bestanden in China zahlreiche Fürstentümer nebeneinander. Jeder Fürstenstaat legte zur Verteidigung seines Territoriums eine Schutzmauer an. Das war der Anfang der Großen Mauer.

221 v. Chr. ließ dann der Qin-Kaiser Shi Huang Di, der Begründer der Qin-Dynastie, der China einigte, diese einzelnen Mauern miteinander verbinden und ausbauen. Zu jener Zeit begann die Große Mauer im Westen bei Lintao, im heutigen Kreis Minxian, Provinz Gansu, verlief in östlicher Richtung durch das heutige Autonome Gebiet Innere Mongolei und die jetzigen Provinzen Shaanxi, Shanxi und Hebei und endete im Ostteil der Provinz Liaoning. In den darauffolgenden Dynastien wurde die Große Mauer dann noch weiter ausgebaut. Die Große Mauer erstreckt sich heute von Jiayuguan in der Provinz Gansu im Westen bis nach Shanhaiguan in der Provinz Hebei im Osten. Sie ist ungefähr 6700 Kilometer lang. Die heute gut erhaltene Große Mauer war hauptsächlich in der Ming-Dynastie gebaut worden. Die Große Mauer ist durchschnittlich 6 bis 7 m hoch und 4 bis 5 m breit.

Heute ist der imponierende Abschnitt der Großen Mauer bei Badaling eine bekannte Sehenswürdigkeit, die zahlreiche im- und ausländische Reisende anzieht. Eine 62 Kilometer lange Autobahn führt von Stadtgebiet Beijings bis zum Teil der Großen Mauer im Gebiet Badaling.

1987 wurde die Große Mauer in die „Liste des Kultur- und Naturerbes der Erde" der UNESCO aufgenommen.

La Grande Muraille a été inscrite, par l'UNESCO, sur la liste des trésors du patrimoine culturel mondial. Partant de la passe Shanhaiguan dans la province du Hebei et aboutissant à la passe Jiayuguan dans la province du Gansu, elle mesure 6 700 km de long. La construction de ce gigantesque ouvrage défensif commença au VIIe siècle av. J.-C. à l'Epoque des Printemps et Automnes et des Royaumes combattants et s'acheva en 221 av. J.-C.. Après avoir unifié la Chine, l'empereur Shihuangdi des Qin entreprit de restaurer, de prolonger et de relier les divers tronçons de murailles érigées par les principautés pour se protéger des incursions des tribus nomades du Nord. Pendant des siècles, des travaux de consolidation et d'extension furent effectués par les dynasties successives. La muraille des Ming, le long de laquelle furent érigées de nombreuses tours d'alarme, s'étendait sur la longueur de la muraille actuelle.

La Grande Muraille à Badaling, le tronçon le plus complet et le mieux conservé, a une hauteur moyenne de 6 à 7 m et une largeur de 4 à 5 m. Une autoroute de 61,87 km, mise en service le 9 novembre 1998, permet de se rendre à Badaling en une heure seulement.

Badaling section of the Great Wall

Die Große Mauer bei Badaling

La Grande Muraille à Badaling

Juyongguan Pass

Die Festung Juyongguan bei Badaling

La Passe Juyongguan.

Juyonguan Pass.   An important pass to Inner Mongolia, the Juyonguan Pass lies about 50 km to the northwest of Beijing. It is slanked on both sides by towering dark green mountains. In the valley, green and luxuriant are the pines and cypresses. It is called "Dark Green Juyong" — one of the "Eight Celebrated Scenic Spots of Yanjing (Beijing)".Renovated on a large scale, what the Chinese and foreign tourists are seeing now is an entirely new Juyongguan Pass.

Der Paß Juyongguan, etwa 50 km nordwestlich von Beijing, war ein wichtiger Durchgang zur Inneren Mongolei. Er liegt nördlich des Bergpasses Nankou und südlich des Bergpasses Badaling in einer 20 Kilometer langen schmalen Schlucht, die zu beiden Seiten von hohen Bergen eingeschlossen ist. Die mit Gras und Blumen bedeckten Berghänge verlaufen wie grüne Wellen.

La passe Juyongguan. Elle se trouve à 50 km au nord-ouest de Beijing. C'est l'une des passes les plus importantes de la Grande Muraille, ouvrant sur la Mongolie intérieure. La Terrasse des Nuages, un des Huit Sites de Yanjing, est environnée de montagnes couvertes d'une végétation luxuriante. Après de grands travaux de restauration, la passe Juyongguan a pris un nouvel aspect.

Great Wall at sunset

Die Große Mauer bei
Sonnenuntergang

La Grande Muraille au
crépuscule.

Winter view of the Badaling section of the Great Wall

Die Große Mauer im Schnee

La Grande Muraille à Badaling en hiver.

Autumn scenery at the Great Wall

Die Große Mauer im Herbst

La Grande Muraille en automne

(*Right*) Watchtower. It was used for shooting and observing.

Alarmfeuerturm *(rechts)* Die Alarmfeuertürme standen meist auf den Gipfeln oder an höher gelegenen Stellen. Kam es zu einem feindlichen Angriff, wurden auf den Alarmfeuertürmen Warnungsfeuer entzündet. Auf diese Weise konnte eine Meldung von Turm zu Turm bis zur Hauptstadt weitergeleitet werden.

La tour d'alarme *(à droite)*. On allumait des feux sur ces tours pour transmettre des messages.

Simatai section of the Great Wall

Die Große Mauer bei Simatai

La Grande Muraille à Simatai.

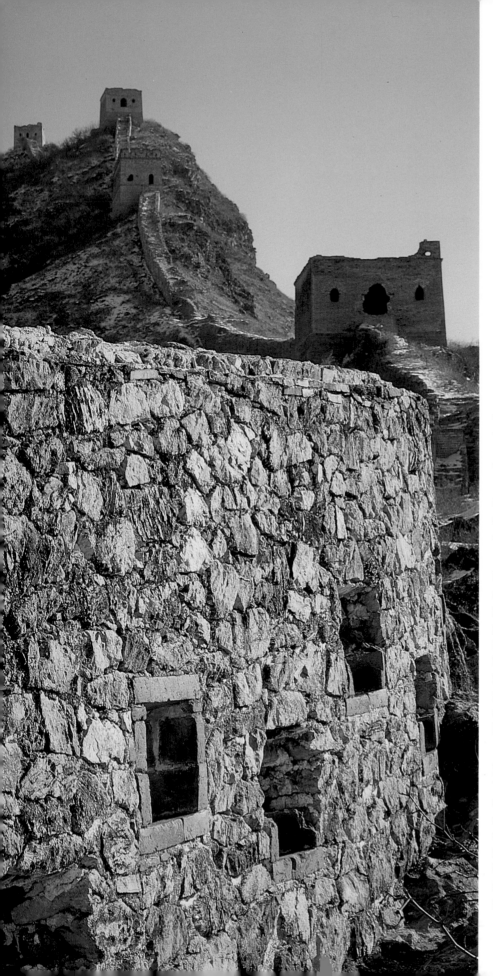

Simatai section of the Great Wall

Die Große Mauer mit Schießecharten in Simatai

La Grande Muraille à Simatai.

(*Right*) Mutianyu section of the Great Wall.   Located 79 km to the northeast of Beijing, the Mutianyu section of the Great Wall is screened by towering mountains, heavily forested and blessed with many natural springs. Natural scene here is exquisitely graceful.

Die Große Mauer bei Mutianyu *(rechts),* 79 km nordöstlich von Beijing, wurde zu Beginn der Ming-Dynastie gebaut. Dieser zwischen hohen und steilen Bergen befindliche Mauerabschnitt ist über 850 km lang, vom Shanhaiguan-Paß bis nach Mutianyu, sowie noch eindrucksvoller als die Badaling-Mauer.

La Grande Muraille à Mutianyu *(à droite)* se trouve à 79 km au nord-est de Beijing. Construit avant 1400, ce tronçon de la Grande Muraille est enserré de deux côtés par de hautes montagnes boisées sur les pentes desquelles coulent des ruisseaux limpides. Le paysage y est plein de charme.

Gate of the Badaling section of the Great Wall

Der Torturm der Badaling-Festung

La porte de la Grande Muraille à Badaling.

Spring scenery at the Great Wall.   In the spring, peach trees are in full bloom. It is the best time to visit the Great Wall.

Die Große Mauer im Frühling

La Grande Muraille au printemps.   Le printemps, au moment de la floraison des pêchers, est la meilleure saison pour escalader la muraille.

Ming Tombs
Die Ming-Gräber
Les Treize Tombeaux des Ming

The Ming Tombs lies at the foot of the Tianshou Mountains, some 50 kilometers to the northwest of Beijing, in a small basin covering an area of 40 square kilometers. They have the Dragon Hill in the east and the Crouching Tiger Hill in the west, lying threateningly on either side of the south entrance. As the tombs of 13 Ming emperors were located here, the Ming Tombs were generally called the 13 Tombs. Entire area of tombs was originally surrounded by a wall with its main entrance at the southern end. During the period of the construction of the necropolis which spanned over 200 years, this was a forbidden area and was heavily guarded.

In early 1956, Chinese Government began the excavation of Dingling Underground Palace, and excavation lasted until in 1958. More than 3,000 pieces of gold, silver, pearl, jade and garments and decorations were unearthed. The Ming Tombs was officially opened to the public in 1959. It is most noted for the magnificent buildings of Changling and the Dingling Underground Palace. From that time on, the Ming Tombs has become a scenic spot for the Chinese and foreign tourists.

Die 13 Ming-Gräber liegen am Fuß des Tianshou-Berges, ungefähr 50 km nordwestlich von Beijing, entfernt. 13 der 16 Kaiser der Ming-Zeit wurden hier bestattet. Der gewaltige Baukomplex dieser Gräbergruppe ist ziemlich vollständig erhalten. Das erste Grab Changling wurde im Jahr 1409 fertiggestellt und das letzte Grab Siling 1644. Es wurde noch in der Qing-Dynastie für den letzten Ming-Kaiser Zhu Youjian gebaut.

Als die Ming-Dynastie im Jahr 1368 begründet wurde, machte Zhu Yuanzhang Nanjing, Provinz Jiangsu, zur Hauptstadt. Als Zhu Di, der dritte Kaiser der Ming-Dynastie, auf den Thron kam, beschloß er, die Hauptstadt nach Beijing zu verlegen. Damit wurde Beijing das Zentrum der Ming-Zeit.

Die Gräber Changling und Dingling sind heute für Besucher zugänglich.

Changling ist das imposanteste Ming-Grab mit drei großen Höfen. Im Grab Dingling wurden der 13. Kaiser der Ming-Dynastie Zhu Yijun und seine beiden Frauen bestattet. 1956 wurde der unterirdische Palast des Grabes Dingling geöffnet. Dabei wurden über 3000 Kulturgegenstände aus Gold und Silber, Jadegegenstände, Perlen und Juwelen sowie Gold- und Silberbarren gefunden.

Les Treize Tombeaux des Ming se trouvent à 50 km au nord-ouest de Beijing, dans une cuvette de 40 km^2 au pied des Monts de la Longévité céleste. Les deux collines, qui se dressent de part et d'autre de l'entrée sud de la nécropole impériale, semblent en protéger l'accès. Treize empereurs des Ming y sont inhumés. La nécropole impériale, entourée à l'origine d'une enceinte s'ouvrait au sud, mais elle est demeurée zone interdite pendant 200 ans.

Au début de 1956, des archéologues chinois ont commencé les fouilles, et ont exhumé, jusqu'en 1958, 3 000 objets précieux d'or, d'argent, de perles, de jade et des vêtements. Les Treize Tombeaux des Ming, site touristique célèbre ouvert au public dès 1959, attirent de nombreux visiteurs en particulier pour l'architecture splendide du tombeau Changling et le palais souterrain du tombeau Dingling.

Stone Animals and Stone Figures.   The Sacred Way is flanked by 12 stone human figures, including military, civil and eunuch officials, and 24 stone animals, including lions, elephants, camels, horses, kirins and xiezhis, all carved out of single blocks of giant stone in 1435 or the 10th year of the reign of Emperor Xuan De of the Ming Dynasty.

Steinstatuen   An beiden Seiten des „Heiligen Weges" stehen zivile und militärische Würdenträger sowie Tiger, Elefanten, Kamele, Pferde und Fabeltiere aus Stein.

Les statues de pierre. Sur les deux côtés de la Voie sacrée, on compte 12 statues de pierre représentant des fonctionnaires militaires et civils et des eunuques, et 24 statues d'animaux: lions, éléphants, chameaux, chevaux et licornes. Elles ont toutes été sculptées en 1435 chacune dans un bloc de pierre.

(*Right*) Sacred Way

Der Heilige Weg *(rechts)*

La Voie sacrée *(à droite)*.

White Marble Arch.　Erected in 1540 or the 19th year of the reign of Emperor Jia Jing of the Ming Dynasty, the White Marble Arch, located at the southernmost end of the Sacred Way, is 28.86 meters wide and 14 meters high. It was vividly carved with kirins, lions, dragons and grotesque animals on its pillars. The upper part of the arch was carved with floating clouds and billowy waves. This large-scale stone arch is a masterpiece of the art of carved stone on the part of working people in the ancient times.

Ehrenbogen　Dieser Marmor-Ehrenbogen am Südende des „Heiligen Wegs" wurde 1540 errichtet. Er ist 28,86 m breit und 14 m hoch. Alle Skulpturen sind aus Marmor graviert.

Le portique ornemental en pierre.　Construit en 1540, il se trouve à l'extrémité sud de la Voie sacrée. Construit en blocs de marbre blanc, ce portique de 28,86 m de large et de 14 m de haut est orné de sculptures représentant des nuages, des vagues, des licornes, des lions, des dragons et d'autres animaux fabuleux. C'est un des chefs-d'œuvre lapidaires de la Chine antique.

Dragon-Headed Turtle Tablet Pavilion.   Inscription on the tablet runs to more than 1,000 characters.

Der Beiting-Pavillon   Im Pavillon steht ein Gedenkstein mit Inschriften. Sein Sockel ist eine Schildkröte aus Stein.

Le Pavillon de la Stèle. Dans le pavillon, une tortue de pierre porte sur son dos une stèle couverte d'inscriptions.

Gate to the Changling
Das Tor des Grabes Changling
L'entrée du tombeau Changling

Minglou (Soul Tower) of Changling. Minglou is the symbol for a tomb. Changling is the first and biggest tomb, which contains the remains of the third Ming Emperor Zhu Di, whose reign lasted from 1403 to 1425. The entire necropolis can be seen from this tower.

Minglou von Changling. Minglou ist das Symbol für ein Grab. Changling ist das erste und auch größte Grab, in dem der dritte Ming-Kaiser Zhu Di (Regierungsperiode 1403-1425) beigesetzt wurde. Vom Turm aus kann man die ganze Totenstadt überblicken.

La Tour de la Stèle du Changling, le premier des Treize Tombeaux des Ming, abrite la dépouille de l'empereur Zhu Di (Yongle).

Ling'en (Prominent Favor) Hall.   Built on a three-tiered marble terrace, the hall covers an area of 1,956 square meters. There are 32 giant unpainted nanmu (a fine hardwood) pillars in the hall, 1.17 meters in diameter and 14.3 meters high. It was once the site to hold sacrificial ceremonies.

Die Ling'en-Halle   Sie befindet sich auf einer dreistöckigen Marmor-Terrasse. Die 32 riesigen Säulen der Halle bestehen jeweils aus einem 14,3 m langen Baumstamm mit einem Durchmesser von 1,17 m. Die Halle nimmt eine Fläche von 1956 m² ein. Hier fanden in alter Zeit Opferzeremonien statt.

La Salle des Faveurs éminentes (Ling'endian). Bâtie sur une triple terrasse de marbre, elle couvre une superficie de 1 956 m². La Salle où étaient organisées les cérémonies du culte est soutenue par 32 gigantesques colonnes de palissandre, dont la plus grande a un diamètre de 1,17 m et une hauteur de 14,3 m.

(*Upper*) Dingling Tomb. Dingling Tomb is the tomb of Zhu Yijun, the 13th emperor of the Ming Dynasty, and two of his concubines (Xiaoduan, Xiaojing).

Das Grab Dingling *(oben)* Zhu Yijun, der 13. Ming-Kaiser, und seine zwei Frauen wurden hier bestattet.

Le tombeau Dingling *(en haut)* abrite les restes du 13e empereur Zhu Yijun et de ses deux épouses.

(*Lower*) Minglou (Soul Tower) in Dingling Tomb

Der Minglou des Dingling *(unten)*

La Tour de la Stèle du tombeau Dingling *(en bas)*.

Baocheng (Precious Wall). This circular wall around the mound is about 750 meters in circumference with crenels on the top. Beneath the mound is the underground palace where the emperor was buried.

Die Mauer der Baocheng (Schatzstadt) Die mit Zinnen versehene Mauer der Schatzstadt ist 750 m lang. Unter der Schatzstadt befindet sich die Grabkammer.

Le chemin de ronde qui enserre le tumulus a une circonférence de 750 m.

Entrance to the Underground Palace

Der Eingang des unterirdischen Palastes des Grabes Dingling

L'entrée du palais souterrain de Dingling.

Passageway of the underground palace

Der unterirdische Durchgang zum unterirdischen Palast

La galerie du palais souterrain.

Dingling Underground Palace.   It covers an area of 1,195 square meters in total, and the height between the top and the ground of the tomb is 27 meters. Two white marble doors are all 3.3 meters high, 1.7 meters wide and about 4 tons in weight. Of the three coffins, the one in middle is for the emperor, and the two others that flank it are for two of his concubines. Surrounding the coffin beds are pieces of jade, flower pots and funerary objects.

Der unterirdische Palast des Grabes Dingling besteht aus 5 Sälen mit einer Gesamtfläche von 1195 m². Sie sind aus Stein erbaut und haben keine Balken oder Säulen. Der Palast ist so tief unter der Erde angelegt, daß zwischen dem Deckengewölbe und der Erdoberfläche ungefähr 27 m liegen. Die Flügel der Türen zwischen dem vorderen, dem mittleren und dem hinteren Saal bestehen aus weißem Marmor. Jeder ist 3,3 m hoch, 1,7 m breit und 4 t. schwer.

La palais souterrain de Dingling   couvre une superficie de 1195 m², et se trouve à 27 m de profondeur. Les deux portes d'entrée en marbre blanc mesurent chacune 3,3 m de haut et 1,7 m de large, et pèsent 4 tonnes. Les deux cercueils de ses épouses flanquent celui de l'empereur entouré d'objets funéraires.

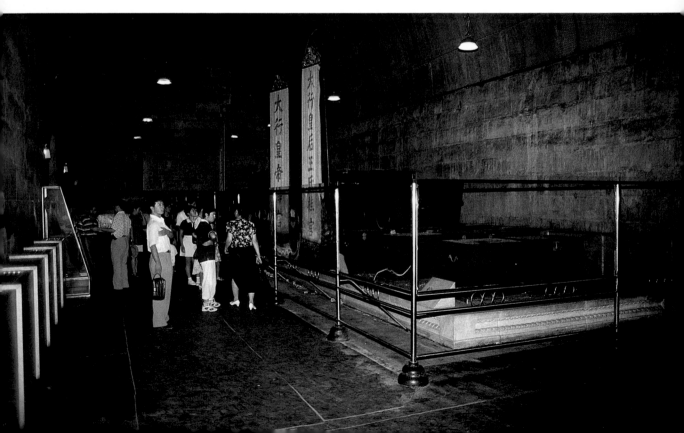

Residence of Prince Gong
Residenz des Prinzen Gong
La Résidence du prince Gong

Residence of Prince Gong refers to the private residence of He Shen (1750-1799), the Grand Secretary of Emperor Qian Long of the Qing Dynasty. When he was in power for 20 years, He Shen left no stone unturned to line his pockets. When Jia Qing ascended the throne, he declared He Shen guilty of a crime of 12 counts and ordered He to kill himself and that He Shen's properties be confiscated. His residence was changed to the Residence of Prince Qing. In 1851, Emperor Xian Feng made his brother Yixin, the Prince of Gong, and gave this place to him. It was bestowed upon Prince Gong as the official residence and the name was changed to the Residence of Prince Gong. The Residence is divided into two parts: living quarters and garden, covering 3.1 and 2.6 hectares respectively.

After Yixin moved in, he built pavilions, dug ponds, made hills and planted trees in the rear part of the residence, turning it into a garden. The garden combines the architectural style of north China with the art of gardening of south China. The general layout of the pavilion, hall, courtyard and building is so complicated and unpredicable that there are so many enchanting scenic spots that we can justifiably rate as the most outstanding example of the antique architecture and art of gardening of China.

Die Residenz des Prinzen Gong war ursprünglich die private Residenz von He Shen, dem großen Sekretär der Qing-Dynastie. Wegen Bestechung wurde er hingerichtet, sein Eigentum wurde beschlagnahmt. Seine Residenz wurde zur Residenz des Prinzen Qing. Im Jahre 1851 verlieh Kaiser Xianfeng an Yixin den Titel „Prinzen Gong" und gab ihm den Palast als Residenz. Die Residenz besteht aus zwei Teilen — Wohngelände und Garten. Das Wohngelände nimmt eine Fläche von 3,1 ha ein und der Garten von 2,6 ha.

Nachdem Yixin seinen Wohnsitz dorthin verlegt hatte, verwandelte er den hinteren Teil der Residenz in einen Garten, in dem er Pavillons bauen, Teiche ausheben, Hügel aufschütten und Bäume pflanzen ließ. Der Garten verbindet den architektonischen Stil in Nordchina mit der Gartenbaukunst von Südchina. Er ist ein hervorragender klassischer Garten.

C'est le jardin princier le mieux conservé de Beijing. Il était à l'époque de l'empereur Qianlong des Qing la résidence de He Shen. Pendant qu'il était au poste de grand lettré, celui-ci était tyrannique et a collectionné une grande fortune. Après qu'il s'était suicidé sur l'ordre de l'empereur Jiaqing des Qing, la résidence devint la propriété du prince Qingwang. En 1851, l'empereur Xianfeng des Qing conféra à son frère cadet Yixin le titre de prince Gongwang et lui donna la résidence du prince Qingwang qui devait alors prendre son nom actuel. La résidence du prince Gongwang est composée de deux parties: 3,1 ha d'habitations, et 2,6 ha de jardin.

Yixin y fit planter des arbres, construire des pavillons, des collines et des lacs artificiels. Son jardin marie les styles architecturaux de la Chine du Sud et de la Chine du Nord et le style des jardins du sud.

Garden of the Residence of Prince Gong

Garten der Residenz des Prinzen Gong

Le jardin de la résidence du prince Gongwang.

Duxiufeng (Peak of Unique Elegance). Yixin, brother of Emperor Xian Feng of the Qing Dynasty, regarded himself supremely noble, so had the character "Unique" carved at the top of the rock. That is where the tablet derives its name.

Duxiufeng Yixin betrachtete sie selbst als besonders vornehm. So ließ er das Schriftzeichen „einzig" in den oberen Teil des Felsen einmeißeln. Deswegen bekam der Fels den Namen Duxiufeng (Gipfel der Alleinstehende Schönheit).

Pic de la Joie solitaire (Duxiufeng). En tant que frère cadet de l'empereur Xianfeng des Qing, Yixin se considérait comme un parent distingué du Fils du Ciel et fit graver sur le rocher le caractère «solitaire».

Bamboo Courtyard.　The courtyard is full of green bamboos, plants and flowers to show the loftiness of its owner.

Bambus-Hof　Der Hof ist neben Blumen und Bäumen voll mit grünem Bambus bepflanzt und zeugt vom Stolz seines Besitzers.

La Cour des Bambous exprime le goût raffiné du propriétaire.

Pavilion for Poetry and Painting.   Built in the center of a pond, it can be reached only by boat.

Pavillon für Poesie und Malerei   Der Pavillon wurde inmitten des Teichs gebaut.

Le kiosque de poésie et de peinture. Construit au milieu de l'étang, les visiteurs doivent prendre un bateau pour y monter.

Theater of the Residence of Prince Gong.　Similar theaters can be found all over the country today. However, it was very rare during the Qing Dynasty.

Das Theater　In der Qing-Zeit gab es ganz wenige Theater dieser Art.

Le théâtre de la résidence du prince Gongwang, exceptionnel à l'époque des Qing, ressemble beaucoup à un théâtre moderne.

Interior of the Theater.　Many palace lanterns are hung in the theater, and the walls are decorated with paintings. The audience can sip tea while enjoying the wonderful performance.

Innenansicht des Theaters　An der Decke hängen viele „Langlebigkeits"-Laternen, und die Wände sind mit Gemälden dekoriert. Während die Besucher in der Halle Tee trinken, werden ihnen Vorführungen geboten.

L'intérieur du théâtre. Dans la salle ornée de lanternes et de peintures murales, les touristes peuvent assister à des représentations tout en buvant du thé.

A corner of the garden

Eine Ecke des Gartens

Un coin du jardin, autrefois appelé Jardin des Ondes limpides (Qingyiyuan).

Yuguan (Elm Pass). On the stone tablet is carved "Purple Cloud Range". Though the pass is small, its design is quite imaginative. It is an imitation of the Great Wall and coordinates from afar with the "Purple Cloud Range" stone tablet at the entrance of the Pass.

Yuguan (Ulmen-Paß) Auf der Steintafel vor Yuguan ist die Inschrift „Paß der Azurblauen Wolken" eingraviert. Der Paß ist eine kleine Imitation der Graßen Mauer.

La Passe de l'Orme (Yuguan). Cette reproduction de la Grande Muraille est pleine d'imagination. Sur une stèle de pierre, on lit «Colline des nuages verts» (Cuiyunling).

Ruins of Yuanmingyuan
Die Ruinen des Yuanmingyuan
Ruines de Yuanmingyuan

Yuanmingyuan, covering an area of 347 hectares, is home to the Garden of Ten Thousand Springs and the Garden of Superb Springs. The construction began in 1709 or the 48th year of the reign of Emperor Kang Xi and was completed in 1744 during the reign of Emperor Qian Long. And it went through the periods of Emperors Jia Qing, Dao Guang and Xian Feng, a span of 150 years. Yuanmingyuan was once praised in the West as the "Best of All Gardens". It was a combination of the scenic spots and historical sites south of the Yangtze River and the European-styled gardened palaces. The collection of books, calligraphy and paintings of the past dynasties in the Yuanmingyuan were of highest artistic value. It is regrettable that this masterpiece of human culture and art was looted, plundered and set afire by the Anglo-French Allied Forces in 1860. As a result, the world-renowned Yuanmingyuan was levelled to the ground. Now, after renovation, the Ruins of Yuanmingyuan has become a place for Chinese and foreign tourists to visit and ponder on the past.

Der Palast Yuanmingyuan bestand aus dem Yuanmingyuan (Garten des Hellen Vollmondes), dem Changchunyuan (Garten des Ewigen Frühlings) und dem Wanchunyuan (Garten des Farbenprächtigen Frühlings). Er nahm eine Fläche von 347 ha ein. Der Bau begann 1709 und nahm insgesamt 150 Jahre in Anspruch.

Der Yuanmingyuan-Palast wurde 1860 und 1900 zuerst von der englisch-französischen Invasionsarmee und dann von der alliierten Invasionsarmee der acht Mächte geplündert und niedergebrannt. Alle Kulturgegenstände und Schätze wurden von den Eindringlingen geraubt. Heute stehen die Ruinen des Yuanmingyuan unter Denkmalschutz und sind zu einem Ausflugsort geworden.

Cet ancien groupe de jardins comprenait le Yuanmingyuan, le Wanchunyuan (Jardin du Printemps millénaire) et le Changchunyuan (Jardin du Printemps perpétuel) et couvrait une superficie de 347 ha. Sa construction, commencée en 1709 sous le règne de l'empereur Kangxi, dura 150 ans.

Appelé «Jardin des Jardins» par les Occidentaux, le Yuanmingyuan mariait le style de la Chine du Sud et le style européen. Il renfermait d'innombrables livres anciens, calligraphies, peintures, objets précieux. Malheureusement, ce chef-d'œuvre a été successivement pillé et incendié par l'Armée anglo-française en 1860 et l'Armée coalisée des Huit Puissances en 1900. Des restaurations sont en cours aujourd'hui.

Remains of the Western-Styled Building. The construction took 12 years (1747—1759) during the reign of Emperor Qian Long of the Qing Dynasty. It was burnt down by the Anglo-French Allied Forces in 1860.

Die Ruinen des Xiyanglou Xiyanglou (das Europäische Gebäude) wurde zwischen 1747-1759 während der Regierungsperiode Qianlong der Qing-Dynastie erbaut.

Ruines du Bâtiment occidental. Construit de 1747 à 1759 sous le règne de l'empereur Qianlong, cette construction fut incendiée en 1860 par l'Armée anglo-française.

Yellow-Flower Battle Array.   This is also known as the Ten-Thousand Flower Battle Array, which is a labyrinth in the Yuanmingyuan.

Der Irrgarten Huanghuazhen

Le labyrinthe dans le Yuanmingyuan.

Ruins of the Garden of Harmony and Super Interest.   It was originally a Western-style complex of buildings.

Die Ruinen von Xieqiqu

Ruines du Jardin de l'Harmonie et de la Rareté (Xieqiqu), de style occidental.

Ruins of the Hall for Sea Food Banquets

Die Ruinen der Haiyantang-Halle

Ruines de la Salle des Banquets de Mer (Haiyantang).

Sea of Happiness. This is the biggest man-made lake in Yuanmingyuan. Scenery on this island is quite enchanting. There was once a scenic spot called "Lotus Island and Precious Jade Stage".

Der Fuhai-See

Le Lac du Bonheur (Fuhai). C'est le plus grand lac artificiel de Yuanmingyuan. Sur l'Île des Lotus, se trouvait une Terrasse de Jade.

Ruins of the Supernatural Abbey.　It was originally a Western-style architecture. Legend has it that the resting place of Princess Fragrant (a Uygur girl who was said to have a sort of queer bodily fragrance with her), a beloved imperial concubine of Emperor Qian Long.

Die Ruinen des Fangwaiguan　Ursprünglich gab es hier ein Gebäude im europäischen Stil, das, wie es heißt, der Palast des uigurischen Mädchens Xiangfei, einer Lieblingskonkubine des Kaisers Qianlong, war.

Ruines du Monde extraordinaire (Fangwaiguan).　Selon la légende, cette construction de style occidental était la résidence d'une favorite de l'empereur Qianlong des Qing. Celle-ci était une Ouïgour et son corps exhalait un parfum particulier.

Yonghegong Lamasery
Yonghegong
La Lamaserie Yonghe

It is located inside the Andingmen in the city's north district. Built in 1694, the Lamasery was originally the residence of Emperor Yong Zheng before he ascended the throne. In 1725, it was renamed Yonghegong. In 1744, Yonghegong was declared a lamasery and it was also a mourning hall for the Qing emperors to worship the images and the memorial tablets of their ancestors.

The Yonghegong Lamasery consists of five main halls and the east and west wing halls. These magnificent buildings possess the architectural features of the Han, Manchu, Mongolian and Tibetan ethnic groups. Of the large number of cultural relics preserved in the lamasery, the most renowned is the statue of Maitreya carved from a single trunk of sandalwood. It is 26 meters high, rising 18 meters above the ground. After 1949 it was listed among the cultural relics subject to priority protection. In 1981, it was again open to the public after repeated renovations and has since become a famous scenic spot for Chinese and foreign visitors.

Yonghegong, das größte Lamakloster in Beijing, liegt innerhalb des Tors Andingmen im Dongcheng-Bezirk der Stadt. Die Anlage entstand im Jahr 1694, diente dem Qing-Kaiser Yongzheng vor seiner Thronbesteigung als Residentz und hieß Yongqinwangfu. Im Jahr 1725 bekam sie den Namen Yonghegong und wurde zu einem Lamakloster umgebaut.

Der ganze Baukomplex besteht aus drei Torbögen, fünf Haupthallen — Tianwangdian, Yonghedian, Yongyoudian, Falundian und Wanfuge — und den ost- und westseitlichen Nebenhallen sowie dem Sixuedian. Diese farbenprächtigen Bauwerke weisen architektonische Merkmale der Han-, mandschurischen, mongolischen und tibetischen Nationalität auf. Unter den zahlreichen Kulturgegenständen ist die 18 m hohe Buddha-Statue aus Sandelholz am bekanntesten. Seit der Gründung der Volksrepublik China steht der Yonghegong unter staatlichem Schutz und ist seit 1981 für Touristen geöffnet.

Construite en 1694 à l'intérieur de la porte Andingmen dans le nord de Beijing, c'était à l'origine la résidence de l'empereur Shizong des Qing avant que celui-ci ne fût monté sur le trône. Il prit son nom actuel de Yonghegong (Palais de la Dignité et de l'Harmonie) en 1725 et devint un temple lamaïque en 1744.

La lamaserie comprend cinq cours successives, bordées de salles latérales. Elle combine les styles architecturaux mongol, chinois, islamique et tibétain. La statue de Bouddha en bois de santal, de 26 m de haut (dont 18 m au-dessus du sol), est très célèbre. Après la Libération de la Chine en 1949, il fut placé sous la protection de l'Etat et devint un site touristique important en 1981 après plusieurs restaurations.

Fa Lun Dian (Hall of Wheel of Law).　The architecture of this hall has the typical architectural style of the lamasery. There are five small pavilions on the golden glazed-tiled roof of Fa Lun Dian. On top of every pavilion there is a small-sized dagoba overlooking the hall, in the shape of a horizontal cross.

Die Falundian (Halle des Buddhistischen Rades) hat den typischen Baustil eines Lama-Klosters. Auf dem Dach der Halle stehen 5 kleine Pavillons, und auf jedem Pavillon befindet sich eine kleine Lama-Pagode.

La Salle de la Roue de la Loi (Falundian). Cette construction au style typiquement lamaïque a un plan en croix et sa toiture est dorée de tuiles vernissées surmontée de cinq petites pagodes.

The archway in front of the lamasery's main entrance

Torbogen vor dem Haupteingang des Klosters

Le portique devant la Lamaserie.

Yonghemen (Gate of Harmony).　It is also called Tianwangdian (Devaraja Hall). Every year during the season of tourism, a continuons stream of Chinese and foreign visitors come to pay visits. Very large incense burners on the east and west side dawdle up coiling insence smoke. The inscriptions on the board hung high in the hall and the couplet were written by Emperor Qian Long himself.

Yonghemen, die Halle der Himmlischen Könige, fasziniert jährlich zahlreiche in- und ausländische Touristen. Die Inschriften auf der horizontalen Tafel und das Spruchpaar in der Halle stammen von der Hand von Kaiser Qianlong.

La Porte de la Dignité et de l'Harmonie (Yonghemen), appelée aussi Salle des Rois célestes (Tianwangdian). La tablette horizontale et les sentences parallèles à l'intérieur de la salle sont calligraphiées par l'empereur Qianlong des Qing.

現妙明心

Bag Buddha.　The Bag Buddha worshipped in the Hall of Heavenly Kings is generally called the Big Belly Maitreya.

Der Würdenträger mit Stofftasche (Buddha Maitreja mit großem Bauch)

Le bouddha Meitreya dans la Salle des Rois célestes (Tianwangdian).

Statue of Skanda.　Standing by the rear gate to the Hall of Heavenly Kings, the statue has vajra in the right hand, and wears a suit of golden armor. He is one of the guardians of Buddhism. It is also called the Guardian General of the Heaven.

Statue von Skanda mit einem Vajra in der Hand steht mit dem Gesicht nach Norden am Hintertor der Halle der Himmlischen Könige.

La statue de Skanda dressée à la porte postérieure de la Salle des Rois célestes.

Yubeiting (Pavilion of the Imperial Stele). There inscribed on the stele four different caligraphies — Manchu, Chinese, Mongolian and Tibetan. Hence the name of the Pavilion of the Four-Caligraphy Stele. They record the origin of Lamaism. The back of the stele bears Chinese characters written by Emperor Qian Long.

Yubeiting Auf der Gedenktafel im Yubeiting stehen Han-, mandschurische, mongolische und tibetische Texte, die den Ursprung des Lamaismus beschreiben. Auf der Rückseite der Gedenktafel steht eine von Kaiser Qianlong geschriebenen Inschrift.

Le Pavillon de la Stèle impériale. La stèle raconte l'histoire du lamaïsme en quatre langues: mandchou, chinois, mongol et tibétain. On trouve aussi une calligraphie de l'empereur Qianlong au dos de la stèle.

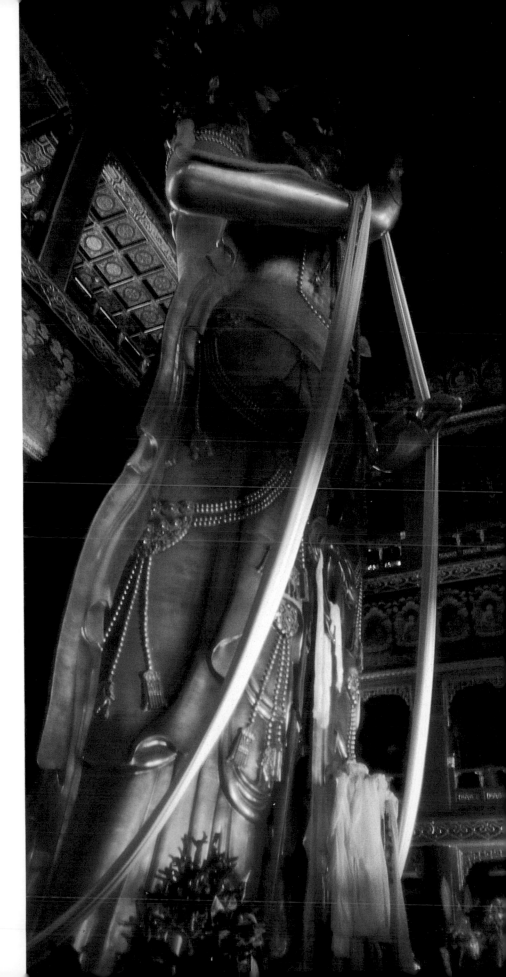

(*Left*) Wanfuge (Hall of Ten Thousand Happiness). It is the largest hall in the lamasery. The white sandalwood statue of Maitreya worshipped in this hall is 26 meters high, rising 18 meters above the ground. With *hada* in hand, the statue looks quite benevolent.

Wanfuge *(links oben)* Der Wanfuge (Pavillon des Zehntausendfachen Glücks) ist die größte Halle des Klosters. In ihr steht die 18 m hohe Buddha-Statue aus Sandelholz.

Le Pavillon des Dix Mille Bonheurs (Wanfuge) *(à gauche)*. C'est la plus grande construction de la lamaserie; elle abrite la fameuse statue de Bouddha de 26 m de haut, dont 18 m au-dessus du sol.

Standing Sandalwood Statue of Maitreya

Die Maitreya-Statue in der Halle der Himmlischen Könige

La statue de Bouddha en santal.

(*Left*)Tibetan-style Four-Faced Buddha in front of the Hall of Eternal Blessing

Buddhafigur vor der Yongyoudian *(links)*

La statue de Bouddha à quatre visage de style tibétain devant
la Salle de la Protection éternelle *(à gauche)*.

Eighteen Arhats. The refers to 18 Arhats worshipped in the Hall of Harmony and Peace

Die achtzehn Arhats in der Halle der Harmonie und des Friedens

Les dix-huit arhats dans la salle principale de la lamaserie.

Yongyoudian (Hall of Eternal Blessing).   Also called Shengyudian (Hall of Imperial Celestial), it was once the place for worshipping the image of Emperor Yong Zheng.

Yongyoudian   Früher stand hier eine Statue von Kaiser Yongzheng.

La Salle de la Protection éternelle (Yongyoudian), où était conservée l'image de l'empereur Yongzheng des Qing.

Great Bell Temple
Dazhongsi
Le Temple de la Grande Cloche

Situated to the north of the Third Ring Road, Dazhongsi or the Great Bell Temple was built in 1733, otherwise called "Temple of Awakening". It derived its name from the Great Bell cast during the reign of Emperor Yong Le of the Ming Dynasty and stored in this temple. The Great Bell Temple was once the place for the emperors to pray for the rain and for the worshippers to conduct Buddhist ceremonies and to make pilgrimage to. The Great Bell is 6.94 meters high and 22 cm thick. Its external diameter is 3.3 meters and weight about 46.5 tons. There were altogether 17 kinds of Buddhist sutras and incantations cast on the inner side and outer side of the bell, more than 227,000 Chinese characters in all. It was measured that the toll of the bell could be heard about 20 kilometers away. Now, this temple has in its collection many ancient bells, great and small, of the past dynasties, open to the Chinese and foreign visitors.

Der Dazhongsi (Tempel der Großen Glocke) liegt an der Dritten Ringstraße von Beijing. Der Tempel, der 1733 in der Regierungsperiode des Kaisers Yongzheng der Qing-Dynastie gebaut wurde, hieß ursprünglich Jueshengsi. Im Tempel hängt es die Yongle-Großglocke, die während der Periode Yongle in der Ming-Zeit gegossen wurde. Diese Glocke ist 6,94 Meter hoch, 22 Zentimeter dick, hat einen 3,3 Meter großen Außendurchmesser und wiegt 46,5 Tonnen. Auf der Innen- und Außenseite des Glockenkörpers stehen kanonische Schriften des Buddhismus — etwa 227 000 Schriftzeichen. Im Tempel sind heute viele Glocken aus allen Zeiten Chinas ausgestellt.

Appelé aussi Temple de l'Eveil (Jueshengsi), il fut construit en 1733 dans le nord de Beijing. Il doit son nom actuel à la grande cloche fondue sous le règne de l'empereur Yongle des Ming, qui mesure 6,94 m de haut, 22 cm d'épaisseur, 3,3 m de diamètre extérieur, pèse 46,5 tonnes environ, et est ornée de 227 000 caractères de soutras. On peut l'entendre sonner à 20 km à la ronde. Aujourd'hui, le temple renferme une collection de cloches de toutes formes et de différentes époques.

Museum of the ancient bells in the Great Bell Temple

Dazhongsi-Museum für antike Glocken

Le Musée de cloches dans le Temple de la Grande Cloche.

Bell Tower.   Situated in the middle of the Great Bell Temple, the tower was built on a green stone foundation, thus a round shape on a square shape, symbolizing "the sky is round and the earth square". It constitutes the most characteristic and extraordinary architecture of the Great Bell Temple.

Der Glockenturm steht im Zentrum des Tempels der Großen Glocke. Er ruht auf einer großen Terrasse aus Stein und hat ein rundes Dach und ein rechteckiges Fundament, was den Himmel und die Erde symbolieren soll.

La tour de la cloche au milieu du temple. Carrée à la base et circulaire à son sommet, elle est bâtie sur des fondations en pierre et symbolise la voûte céleste et la terre carrée.

(*Upper left*) Big Bell of Yong Le. The big bell is 6.94 meters high and 22 cm thick. Its external diameter is 3.3 meters, and the weight about 46.5 tons. There were altogether 17 kinds of Buddhist sutras and incantations cast on the inner side and outer side of the bell, more than 227,000 Chinese characters in all.

Die Yongle-Glocke (*oben links*)

La Grande Cloche Yongle (*en haut à gauche*), de 6,94 m de haut, portant 227 000 caractères de soutras bouddhiques.

(*Upper right*) Great Bell for the appreciation of the visitors

Große Glocke (*oben rechts*)

Une grande cloche pour l'appréciation des visiteurs. (*en haut à droite*)

Interior of the Great Bell Temple

Innenansicht des Tempels der Großen Glocke

Le Temple de la Grande Cloche.

Morning Bell.   This bell was exquisitely and beautifully molded. In the middle of the geometrical design on the bell board were carved a lifelike dragon mounting the surrounding clouds and riding the mist. This is really a perfect masterpiece.

Chao-Glocke   Mit ihrer exquisiten Form und den Drachen als Verzierung ist diese Glocke ein hervorragendes Kunstwerk aus der Qing-Zeit.

La cloche de la cour impériale. Ce chef-d'œuvre artistique est orné de figures géométriques et de dragons volant dans les nuages.

Fragrant Hills Park
Xiangshan-Park
La Colline parfumée

The Fragrant Hills lies more than 20 kilometers to the northwest of Beijing. Its peaks rise one higher than the other. It is blessed also with many clear murmuring streams. Densely forested, the landscape is pretty. Emperors of Jin, Yuan, Ming and Qing dynasties, especially in the 10th year of the reign of Emperor Qian Long of the Qing Dynasty, constructed pavilions, platforms, buildings and storeyed pavilions here, 28 scenic spots altogether and named Jingyiyuan (Garden of Ease and Quiet). It was destroyed twice in 1860 and 1900. Completely renovated after 1949, it is open to the public as the Fragrant Hills Park.The park is quiet and beautiful, with enchanting scenery. In late autumn, Chinese and foreign visitors come here to enjoy maple tree leaves. That is something they are longing for. Spectacles Lake, Jianxinzhai (Pavilion of Revealing One's Mind), Zhaomiao (Luminous Temple), Incence Burner Peak, Shuanqing (Twin Clear Waters) and Glazed-Tiled Pagoda are the best scenic spots in the park.

Biyunsi (Temple of Azure Clouds) and Wofosi (Temple of Reclining Buddha) are the next-door neighbors of Park. In the Biyunsi, the most famous buildings are the Hall of Arhats carved out of hardwood and decorated in gold foil and the Diamond Throne Pagoda. In Wofosi, there are many towering ancient cypresses and out of it, there are crystal clear streams. Visitors come here to enjoy the pleasure of quietness.

Der Xiangshan (Duftender Berg)-Park liegt 20 Kilometer nordwestlich vom Stadtteil Beijings entfernt.

Im Park stehen viele Sehenswürdigkeiten wie Paläste, Tempel, Pavillons und Pagoden aus der Jin-, Yuan-, Ming- und Qing-Zeit. 1860 und 1900 wurden die Bauwerke zerstört. Nach der Gründung der Volksrepublik China wurden sie mehrmals restauriert, wobei sie ihre originale Gestalt wieder erhielten.

Ce beau parc se situe à 20 km au nord-ouest de la ville de Beijing. Des constructions y furent aménagées sous les dynasties des Jin, des Yuan, des Ming et des Qing. En 1745 sous le règne de l'empereur Qianlong des Qing, la réalisation de 28 sites pittoresques était achevée et on le nomma Jardin de la Tranquillité et du Plaisir (Jingyiyuan). Détruit successivement en 1860 et 1900, ce parc a été complètement restauré après 1949.

Jianxinzhai (Pavilion of Revealing One's Mind).   It was built during the reign of Emperor Jia Jing of the Ming Dynasty. In the center of this exquisite small courtyard is a semi-circular pond, by whose west side stands the three-room Pavilion of Relieving One's Mind. Behind the pavilion stands dark green ancient pines and cyprsses and lies jagged rocks of grotesque shapes. The environment makes the courtyard even more quiet and tasteful.

Jianxinzhai (Pavillon der Offenbarung des Gemütes) aus der Qing-Zeit ist ein exquisit gestalteter Hof im Baustil eines südchinesischen Gartens. Im Zentrum des Hofes befindet sich ein Teich, und hinter dem Hof stehen viele alte Kiefern und Zypressen sowie seltsam geformte Felsen.

Le Pavillon de l'Introspection (Jianxinzhai). Construit à l'époque de l'empereur Jiajing des Ming, il se dresse au bord d'un étang semi-circulaire et devant des cyprès verdoyants et des rochers aux formes déchiquetées.

(*Right*) Fragran Hills Hotel.   Designed by the world-renowned Chinese-American architect I. M. Pei, the hotel has a quite simple and refined surrounding.

Xiangshan-Hotel *(rechts)* — ein modernes Hotel in herrlicher Umgebung

L'Hôtel de la Colline parfumée *(à droite)*, œuvre de Leoh Ming Pei, célèbre architecte américain d'origine chinoise.

(*Upper*) Shuangqing Villa (Villa of Twin Clear Waters). Two crystal clear streams flows out of stone cracks into a pond on whose side stands a very pretty pavilion.

Die Shuangqing-Villa in malerischer Umgebung (oben)

La Villa aux Deux Sources limpides «Shuangqingbieshu) *(en haut)*. Au bord de l'étang alimenté par deux sources, se dresse un pavillon élégant.

Fragrant Hills Park in Autumn.   Maple tree leaves are over hill and dale.
That is what the Chinese and foreign visitors are longing to enjoy the sight of.

Der Xiangshan-Park im Herbst

La Colline parfumée en automne.

Glazed-Tiled Pagoda. This is an octagonal and seven-storeyed pagoda built with colored glazed tiles. The pagoda has 56 bronze bells dangling from its octagonal eaves at every storey.When caressed by a puff of breeze, the bells ring melodiously. It is very poetic.

Liulita (Pagode aus glasierten Ziegeln) ist ein siebenstöckiges und achteckiges Bauwerk. An jeder Ecke hängt eine Bronzeglocke.

La Pagode vernissé. Cette pagode octogonale de sept étages est couverte de céramiques vernissées. Les clochettes au-dessous des avant-toits sonnent mélodieusement au vent.

Stone archway of Biyunsi

Torbogen vor dem Biyunsi

Le portique de pierre du Temple des Nuages d'Azur.

(*Right*) Diamond Throne Pagoda.   Also known as the Temple of Jade Pagoda, it was built with white marble in a shape similar to that of an Indian dagoba. But its structure and carving skill are in the traditionally Chinese style. It looks quite magnificent.

Jingangbaozuo-Pagode *(rechts)*   Die Pagode (Vajra-Stupa auf einem Sockel mit buddhistischen Basreliefs) steht im Biyunsi (Tempel der Azurblauen Wolken). Das Bauwerk aus weißem Marmor ist mit feinen Reliefs verziert und zeigt eine hervorradende Architektur.

La Pagode du Trône de Diamant dans le Temple des Nuages d'Azur *(à droite)*. Cette construction de marbre blanc est de style indien, mais sa structure et ses sculptures sont bien chinoises.

(*Upper*) Hall of Arhats.　There are altogether 508 arhats carved out of hardwood and decorated in gold foil in the hall. Each of them is portrayed to the life in a different pose and with a different expression.

Die Arhats-Halle *(oben)*　beherbergt insgesamt 508 mit Goldfolie überzogene Arhats aus Hartholz. Alle Figuren haben unterschiedliche Haltungen und einen unterschiedlichen Gesichtsausdruck.

La Salle des Arhats *(en haut)*. On y compte 508 statues de bois doré, toutes différentes.

(*Left and right*) Diamond Warriors as Guardian Celestials.　The shape is lifelike and the lines manifest ease and grace. Because one marshall opens the mouth and the other closes, they are also called Marshalls Heng and Ha.

Die Götterfiguren „Ha" *(links)* und „Heng" *(rechts)*

Les gardiens célestes.　Comme l'un d'eux a la bouche fermée et l'autre la bouche ouverte, on les appelle familièrement «les Généraux Hm et Ha».

Fangsheng (Buying captive fish and setting them free)Pool in the Temple of Recumbent Buddha

Der Fangsheng-Teich im Tempel des Schlafenden Buddhas

L'Etant des animaux aquatiques relâchés dans le Temple du Bouddha couché.

Statue of Recumbent Buddha.   Cast out of copper in 1321, the statue weighs 54 tons and is more than 5 meters in length. Its unadorned beauty and exquisiteness fully embody China's ancient casting technique.

Statue des Schlafenden Buddhas   Diese im Jahre 1321 gegossene Statue aus Bronze wiegt 54 Tonnen und ist 5 Meter lang.

Le Bouddha couché.   Coulé en bronze en 1321, il mesure 5 m de long et pèse 54 tonnes.

Beijing in a Nutshell
Beijing im Fokus
Beijing et ses merveilles

Tian'anmen
Das Tian'anmen-Tor
La Porte Tian'anmen

Ming Tombs
Die Ming-Gräber
Les Treize Tombeaux
des Ming

Palace Museum
Der Kaiserpalast
Le Palais impérial

Residence of Prince Gong
Residenz des Prinzen Gong
La Résidence du prince Gong

Beihai Park
Der Beihai-Park
Le parc Beihai

Ruins of Yuanmingyuan
Die Ruinen des
Yuanmingyuan
Ruines de Yuanmingyuan

Summer Palace
Der Sommerpalast
Le Palais d'Eté

Yonghegong Lamasery
Yonghegong
La Lamaserie Yonghe

Temple of Heaven
Der Himmelstempel
Le Temple du Ciel

Great Bell Temple
Dazhongsi
Le Temple de la Grande
Cloche

Grand View Gaden
Daguanyuan
Le Jardin aux Spectacles
grandioses

Fragrant Hills Park
Xiangshan-Park
La Colline parfumée

Great Wall
Die Große Mauer
La Grande Muraille

名誉编辑：李福瀛　段应合
编　　辑：张大明
编　　审：吴显林
责任编辑：王兆辉
摄　　影：赵　军、李维深、杨福生
译　　审：舒　君（英）
　　　　　李道斌（德）
　　　　　吕志祥（法）
装帧设计：郭子芳
封面设计：徐沪生
电脑制作：卢一凡

图书在版编目（CIP）数据

美丽的北京：英文、德文、法文版／张大明编；赵军等摄 .－
北京：海洋出版社，2000.8
　　ISBN 7-5027-4762-1

　　I. 美…　II. ①张…　②赵…　III. 名胜古迹－北京－摄影集
IV. K928.701-64

中国版本图书馆 CIP 数据核字(1999)第 16080 号

海洋出版社 出版发行
（100081　北京市海淀区大慧寺路 8 号）
新 华 书 店 经 销
北京新华彩印厂印刷　　　新华书店发行所经销
2000 年 8 月第 1 版　　2000 年 8 月北京第 1 次印刷
开本：787×1092 1/16　　印张：9.
字数：30 千字　　印数：1～10000 册
05000
海洋版图书印，装错误可随时退换